In Search Of Christmas

A Collection Of Congregational Resources For Thanksgiving, Advent, And Christmas

Elizabeth Morris-Pier

Stephen A. Berger

Eulonda A. Dreher

Russell W. Dalton

D. Andrew Richardson

Jeanne Mueller and Judith Hale Wood

Ellen and James Edgar

CSS Publishing Company, Inc., Lima, Ohio

IN SEARCH OF CHRISTMAS

Some scripture quotations are from the *Revised Standard Version of the Bible*, copyrighted 1946, 1952 ©, 1971, 1973, by the Division of Christian Education of the National Council of the Churches of Christ in the USA. Used by permission.

Some scripture quotations are from the *Holy Bible, New International Version*. Copyright © 1973, 1978, 1984 International Bible Society. Used by permission of Zondervan Bible Publishers. All rights reserved.

"In The Beginning" from "Mother Earth" by Miriam Therese Winter, from *Woman Prayer/Woman Song* by Miriam Therese Winter, copyright © 1987 Medical Mission Sisters, Hartford, Connecticut. Reprinted by permission.

"The Birth of Christ" from *Life Of The Virgin Mary* by Rainer Maria Rilke, edited/translated by C. F. MacIntyre, copyright © 1947 The Regents of the University of California. Reprinted by permission.

"Christ Climbed Down" by Lawrence Ferlinghetti, from *A Coney Island Of The Mind*, copyright © 1958 by Lawrence Ferlinghetti. Reprinted by permission of New Directions Publishing Corp.

For more information about CSS Publishing Company, Inc., resources, visit our website at www.csspub.com or e-mail us at custserv@csspub.com or call (800) 241-4056.

ISBN 0-7880-1916-3   PRINTED IN U.S.A.

Table Of Contents

Come!
See What
God Has Done

A Thanksgiving Event For Children

Jeanne Mueller

and

Judith Hale Wood

Contents

Introduction

Come! See What God Has Done has been designed to make children aware of God's many blessings so often taken for granted. Experiences and activities included in this program focus on Families, God's World of Nature, Our Religious Heritage, Food, Friendships and Fun Times, and Our Bodies and Senses.

A guide sheet for each activity center includes:
1. Activity center title with suggestions for creating an appropriate environment.
2. Scripture verse to be displayed on tagboard at the activity center.
3. Guided learning experience which provides an opportunity for the children to share their personal thoughts and feelings.
4. Several follow-up activities to choose from according to preference, time schedule, or available materials.
5. Closing prayer to be used with each group at the conclusion of the activity.

This Thanksgiving Event was developed to last approximately 75 minutes and to include children in kindergarten through grade six. The time period is adjustable, and older or younger children could be included. Although the Thanksgiving Event was designed for use with church school teachers and their children, parents could be invited to attend, thus making it an intergenerational event.

The first hour is spent in ten-minute segments at each of the six activity centers. The final minutes can be a gathering together of the entire group for some singing and a closing prayer.

The Thanksgiving Event will function smoothly if each class is grouped together and moves as a class from center to center according to the time allowed.

At the beginning each child is given a paper turkey without any feathers. As each activity center is completed, the child receives a feather representing that particular activity which is stapled on his turkey. At the end of the Event, the turkeys should be complete with feathers.

Poster Ideas For Various Centers

I

II

III

IV

Bless This House

Description of Activity Center
    On poster board display magazine pictures of families working and playing together.

Scripture Verse
    Come see what God has done, his wonderful acts among men. (Psalm 66:5)

Guided Learning Experience
    Discuss family life with the children by asking:
    1. What are some things families do together?
    2. What problems do families sometimes have?
    3. What joys do families share?
    4. Why do you suppose God gives us families?
    5. What is special about your family?

Follow-up Activities
A. Nut Family Plaque
    On a 6" by 8" piece of wood or heavy cardboard, glue a nut (walnut, pecan, almond, hazelnut, peanut) — one for each member of your family. With plastic eyes and bits of material and yarn, decorate nuts to be representative of your family. Add BLESS THIS HOUSE in alphabet cereal or alphabet noodles. Thank God for your family.

B. Indian Corn and Feather Place Card

Use a 4" by 6" rectangle of paper. Fold in half. Add turkey body, feathers for tail and peppercorn for eye. Glue on Indian corn and guest's name.

C. Thanksgiving Card

Make a Thanksgiving card showing something you are thankful for and add the following verse:

> *My dad is good;*
> *My mom is kind.*
> *They are the best*
> *That I'll ever find.*

Closing Prayer

Our Heavenly Father, we thank you for giving us a family.

We thank you for moms who hug us, bake us cookies, and care for us when we are sick.

We thank you for dads who work hard every day, love us, and help us with our homework.

Help us to be a kind and loving member of our family. Amen.

Nature's Nook

Description of Activity Center

Collect and display some pictures showing the beauty of God's natural world. Arrange any of the following for the children to explore: seeds, insects, pine cones, acorns, gourds, pumpkins, Indian corn, thistles, wheat, pods.

Scripture Verse

I will praise you, Lord, with all my heart; I will tell of all the wonderful things you have done. (Psalm 9:1)

Guided Learning Experience

If you could pick your favorite season, which one would it be? Why?

For the following activity, speak slowly so that the children will have an opportunity to paint a mental picture.

CLOSE YOUR EYES and think about a time in summer when you were so very hot. Your skin was all sticky and sweaty. Then think of how you felt when you jumped into a cool stream of water — how cool you felt.

Now think about wintertime. It has snowed and the tree branches and bushes are covered with snow. Icicles hang from the roof. Your nose and cheeks are so cold that they tingle. You have lots of fun sledding and making snowballs.

Think again of autumn. The sun is warm. The leaves on the trees are bright red and yellow. The leaves on the ground rustle as you walk in them. You have raked and raked and have a huge pile of leaves. Then you and a friend jump and roll in the pile of leaves. What fun!

Think of one more season — it's spring. Some days the ground is still frozen and hard. You've seen two birds building a nest in the tree outside your window in preparation for the baby birds soon to come. Pussy willows are in bloom in your yard. And then it happens! One day you see a tiny green shoot appear in the garden. Several days later — there are purple and yellow crocuses blooming in your hard.

Most of the things we have thought about are gifts from God — things that we can't buy; things that God gives us — water, sunshine, birds, and trees.

Can you think of three other things that God gives you that you can't buy?

A. Thanksgiving Tree

Draw around your hand three times on colored paper.

Print what you are thankful for on the hands.

Cut out the hands and past them on the tree.

B. Nature Collage

Children combine natural materials to create a collage and add the scripture passage from Psalm 9:1.

C. Gourd Creatures

Children can use natural materials (berries, acorns, cranberries, popcorn, dried flowers), markers, feathers, and buttons to create a Gourd Creature.

Closing Prayer

God, our Creature, we thank you for the beautiful and wonderful world you have created. Especially we thank you for the seasons, for sunshine and rain, for trees to climb and streams to play in. Help us to care for and wisely use these gifts you have given us. Amen.

God Gives; We Give Thanks

Description of Activity Center

Appropriate items related to this center would include a Bible, the church hymnal, a cross, the communion cup, and bread.

Scripture Verse

Let us come before him with thanksgiving and sing joyful songs of praise. (Psalm 95:2)

Guided Learning Experience

Help the children to think about giving and receiving and what God has given to his people.
1. What is the neatest gift you have ever received?
2. What is the nicest gift you have ever given?
3. What do you think is the greatest gift God has ever given?
4. What is the greatest gift you can give God?

Talk with the children about the symbolism and meaning of each of the items displayed.

Suggested Activities

A. Pyramid of Thanks

In each section of the pyramid, the children should place something which reminds them of their religious heritage. Suggestions include a picture of their church, a cross, a Bible, and a picture of Christ. (Pattern for pyramid is included.)

B. Give Thanks Centerpiece

Each child traces his/her hand on folded construction paper. Cut them out, leaving the middle fingers attached. Print or have available a copy of the grace printed below to add to the hands. Encourage the use of the grace at mealtime.

To God who gives us daily bread
  A thankful song we raise,
And pray that he who sends us food
  Will fill our hearts with praise.

C. Church Symbol Silhouette

Cover an area with newspapers. Cut an arch-shaped panel from dark construction paper. Children choose a cardboard pattern of a church, cross, or folded hands. Place the pattern on the paper and, using thinned white poster paint in a spray bottle, "spatter paint" the symbol.

Closing Prayer

Loving God, we thank you for our church, for our teachers and pastor who help us learn about you and your ways, and most of all, for sending us your Son Jesus who taught us to love one another. Help each of us become the best person we can be. Amen.

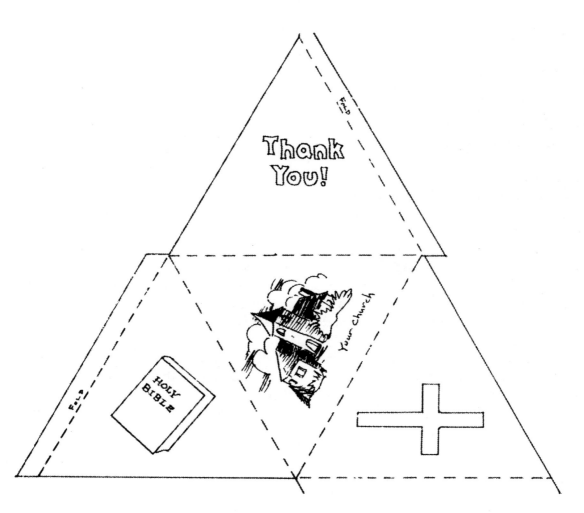

17

Food, Fabulous Food

Description of Activity Center

A cornucopia filled with fruits makes an ideal centerpiece for this center.

Scripture Verse

The land has produced its harvest; God, our God, has blessed us. (Psalm 67:6)

Guided Learning Experience

Ask what the cornucopia represents and then begin the conversation about food by asking:

1. What is your favorite place to eat?
2. What is your favorite food?
3. What is the most special meal you can remember?

Listen to this story and be ready to tell how you would feel if you were the mother, the father, or God.

Once upon a time there was a little girl named Terrible Liz. Her name was Terrible because she was terrible. When she played, she always insisted on her own way. When she left her room, it always looked like a disaster area. If she met you outside she would say, "Where did you get those horrible looking pants?" or "What in the world did you do to your hair?"

But the time she was at her worst was at mealtime. After her dad had worked hard at his job, after Mom had gone grocery shopping and cooked dinner, Terrible Liz could be heard to say, "Oh, no, not that stuff again," or "You know I hate string beans, why do you fix them?" or "Yuk, I'm not eating any squash!" or "Why can't you ever fix something I like?"

Well, that's the way Terrible Liz talked and acted. Let's think about some people that Liz didn't consider.

18

1. How do you think Mom felt after she had shopped and fixed dinner?
2. Why did Dad go to work?
3. Where did the food come from?
4. What things did Terrible Liz do to show that she wasn't thankful to her parents and to God?

Suggested Activities
A. Turkey Shapes

Cut turkey shapes from bread with a cookie cutter. Children can spread them with peanut butter that has been thinned with milk. Decorate with raisin eyes and jelly tails.

B. Harvest Bowl

Children may help prepare the fruits and mix them.

    2 apples peeled, cored, and diced
    a bunch of grapes
    2 handfuls of nuts
    2 handfuls of raisins
    granola cereal

Mix fruits and nuts. Add 2 tablespoons of honey. Sprinkle with granola.

C. Pilgrim Cornbread

The Indians introduced corn to the Pilgrims. Cornbread has become a traditional Thanksgiving dish.

    2 cups cornmeal
    2 teaspoons of baking powder
    1 egg beaten
    1 cup milk
    2 tablespoons of oil
    2 tablespoons of sugar
    1/2 teaspoon of salt

Sift dry ingredients. Add milk, oil, egg, and sugar. Mix well. Pour into greased 8-inch square pan. Bake at 400 degrees for 35 minutes.

Closing Prayer

God, our provider, help us to be thankful for all the food you have given us, not just those foods we like. Help us to remember that there are many in our world who go to bed hungry. We thank you for our food and also for the people who work so that we may eat. Amen.

Friendship And Fun

Description of Activity Center

A collage of children's faces can be displayed with sports equipment, games, and dolls. Add a graffiti board that is titled, A FRIEND IS ... Since this center involves a storytelling experience, plan a special area such as a tent or blanket in a quiet corner.

Scripture Verse

Happy are those who work for peace; God will call them his children! (Matthew 5:9)

Guided Learning Experience

Stir up children's thinking by asking:
1. What makes a good friend?
2. What qualities of a good friend do you have?
3. What can you tell about people by just looking at them?

Have children add their own thoughts and feelings to the graffiti board.

Suggested Activity

The public library has a wealth of good books/stories about friends and friendship. A highly recommended story with a Thanksgiving theme is *Cranberry Thanksgiving* by Wende and Harry Devlin (Parents Magazine Press, 1971).

Cranberry Thanksgiving is a delightful tale of two friends, Maggie and Mr. Whiskers, and a famous cranberry bread recipe. If using this story, be sure to serve some cranberry bread or muffins to the children after the story is told.

Closing Prayer

Almighty God, we thank you for all the special friends we have, for the good times we have playing and sharing with our friends. We know so well how we like our friends to treat us. Help us to be patient, kind, and loving, not only to our friends but also to those who are unfriendly toward us. Amen.

Wonderfully Made

Description of Activity Center

Display a large sheet of white mural paper with this adapted verse from Psalm 47:1 — "O, you children, Clap your hands, Praise the Lord!" Children are to paint one of their hands with various colors of poster paint and then press them on the mural paper to make a collage of handprints.

Also display the Wonderfully Made poster which can be used to introduce the activities.

Scripture Verse

I will give thanks to the Lord with my whole heart. (Psalm 9:1)

Guided Learning Experience

See if the children can name their five senses. Ask them to share with one another:
1. The sweetest/foulest smell they have ever smelled.
2. The hottest/coldest thing they have ever felt.
3. The prettiest/ugliest thing they have ever seen.
4. The loudest/softest thing they have ever heard.
5. The best/worst thing they have ever tasted.

God has given us wonderfully created bodies that we often take for granted. Think of how difficult life would be if part of one's body didn't function properly. We should care for our bodies by seeing that we eat properly, exercise regularly, and avoid things (drugs, alcohol, tobacco) that can harm what God has given us.

Suggested Activities

Prepare the following "sense testers" for the children to experience and then identify.

A. Smell

In small bottles place several drops of peppermint extract, some peanut butter, coffee, vanilla extract, and vinegar for the children to smell.

B. Hear

Tape the following sounds for the children to recognize: a zipper, a door slamming, a telephone ring, a motor starting up (car).

C. Taste

Provide each child with a small taste of each of the following to be identified: salt, lemon, banana, celery, and M & M's.

D. Feel

In small paper bags place the following items: some cotton, a spool, a cookie cutter, a sponge, and a rock. Staple the bags shut and number them. Have the children feel the bag and identify the contents.

Closing Prayer

Dear God, our Creator, you have provided us with a wonderfully-made body. Help us to use our mouths to say kind things, to use our hands in loving and helpful ways, to use our eyes to see beauty in your world, and to use our ears to hear pleasant sounds. May our hearts be filled with love and our actions show that we are truly your children. Amen.

A
Chrismon
Service

Ellen and James Edgar

Revised. Originally published in 1981 as *A Chrismon Service*, copyright © 1981, by CSS Publishing Company, Lima, Ohio (0-89536-500-6).

Introduction

Christmas is a time of expectation and wonder, of pageants and carols, of gift giving and making things. We have tried to incorporate all of these elements in this Chrismon Service.

This Chrismon Service originated with the request of a number of First Presybterian Church women to make Chrismons. Chrismons or symbols for Jesus Christ made in the form of Christmas ornaments are the creation of Mrs. Frances Kipp Spencer and the Lutheran Church of the Ascension, Danville, Virginia. Our women began their work in the summer of 1978.

Once the symbols were made, it was necessary to create a service incorporating their meaning. We consulted a number of area churches who have Chrismon Trees. All used an evening program closely patterned after "The Child We Honor" contained in Mrs. Spencer's *Chrismons Basic Series*. We are especially indebted to Mrs. Spencer for her program and have incorporated much of her material in the service, including the essential congregational participation. We share the common message of proclaiming Jesus the Christ.

The purpose of the service is to portray the drama of redemption. The journey to Bethlehem is also a journey to Calvary and ultimately to heaven. It is a journey from self to God. With this thought in mind we followed the three major categories the Chrismons represent: birth, death and resurrection, and the victorious Christ. At the same time we kept the major movements of worship.

Because the Chrismon Service was designed as an act of worship and properly conducted in the sanctuary, congregational participation is essential. This was accomplished by a number of devotional responses throughout the service, by distributing Chrismons to the congregation, and the presentation of Chrismons at appropriate times in the service. The presentation of the Chrismons represents the gifts we bring to the Christ and forms the central theme of the service. The traditional Offertory is omitted and offering plates are placed at the entrance to the sanctuary to receive the weekly envelopes. The service is a litany of gift giving.

Appropriate Bible passages referring to the symbols were selected from the *Revised Standard Version of the Bible* (1952). Prayers have been revised from the United Presbyterian *Worship Book* (1972).

Because Handel's *Messiah* follows a similar movement, it seemed natural to select portions of the *Messiah* for the service. The music was meant to convey a sense of the awesome grandeur of heaven blended with the simple rejoicing of village folk.

Christmas is more than the simple enchantment of a stable. It is the panorama of salvation. It is both personal and cosmic in scope. Christmas celebrates the day when "the Lord God omnipotent reigneth." We hope these various elements convey a sense of Christmas worship to be experienced in sight, sound, and participation.

Mrs. Spencer, originator of Chrismon ornaments, has given all rights to the Lutheran Church of the Ascension, 314 West Main Street, Danville, Virginia 24541. This church owns the Trademark and Copyrights. Persons interested in learning more about Chrismons should write to the church.

Mrs. Spencer has written that "Chrismons can be an act of worship." We have found it to be so and invite you to find it to be so for yourselves.

Ellen and James Edgar

A Chrismon Service

Organ Prelude   "A Lovely Rose Is Blooming" (Brahms)

Introit   "What Child Is This?" (Greensleeves)

Call to Worship
Pastor: Let us worship God. *For God so loved the world that he gave his only Son, that whoso-ever believes in him should not perish but have eternal life.* (John 3:16)
              Let us praise the Lord.

Processional Hymn   "O Come, All Ye Faithful"
(Two persons will distribute Chrismons to those people sitting at the ends of the pews on the center aisle. At appropriate times in the service these persons with their Chrismons will be asked to come forward to the tree and present their Chrismons to two decorators who will place them on the tree.)

Christmas Confession (in unison)
Almighty God, who sent a star to guide men to the holy child Jesus, we confess we have not always followed the light of your Word. We have not searched for signs of your love in the world. We have failed to praise your Son's birth, and refused his peace on earth. We have questioned the good news. We have expected little and hoped for less. Forgive us, Lord, for such self-serving symbols that mark our lives. Open our hearts to your abiding presence. May the joy of the angels become our joy. May the devotion of the shepherds become our devotion. May the vision of the Wise Men become our vision. May the wonder of your love be born in us, through Jesus Christ, our Lord. Amen.

Declaration of Good News
Pastor: Hear the good news which we receive, in which we stand, and by which we are saved: That Jesus Christ was born, lived, and died for our sins according to the Scriptures; that he was buried, that he was raised on the third day; and that he appeared to the women, to Peter, then to the Twelve, and to many faithful witnesses. We believe he is the Christ, the Son of the living God. He is our Savior, the Victor over the powers of sin and death. He is the first and the last, the beginning and the end. He is our Lord and our God.
People: Amen.
          Be born in us, O Lord. Be born in every part of our lives. Be born in every place where we live, until we are conscious of your presence: In our joys and sorrows. In our fears and our failures. In our hopes and our dreams. In our work and in our worship. Be born in us, O Lord, be born in us this day.
Pastor: Amen.

Hymn of Rejoicing   "Good Christian Friends, Rejoice"

Introduction to Chrismons

At Christmas, not only does the star lead us to Bethlehem, but also Nazareth, Galilee, Capernaum, Jerusalem, Calvary, and heaven. For as part of Jesus' birth, we also celebrate his life and ministry, his death and resurrection, and his ultimate victory over the powers of sin and death.

Like the three kings, we present our gifts to Jesus and to one another. Today we will present our offerings in the form of CHRISMONS. CHRISMON is a combination of two words: CHRIST and MONogram. A Chrismon is a symbol of Christ.

Christian symbols date back to the early church. They are found on the walls of the Roman catacombs, on jewelry and utensils from excavations in Palestine and elsewhere. Early Christians used them to identify themselves to one another, to designate meeting places, and sometimes, to show nonbelievers where they stood. These symbols of the early church served to transmit the faith and beliefs of the followers of Jesus Christ.

Chrismons were first used in 1957 to decorate a Christmas tree in the Lutheran Church of the Ascension in Danville, Virginia. They were composed of white and gold materials. WHITE is symbolic of our Lord's purity and perfection, GOLD, of his majesty, glory, and triumph. The green balsam is symbolic of promised healing. The little white lights on the tree point to the Christ as the light of the world.

Each Chrismon is described in Scripture and refers to some aspect of Jesus Christ. As the particular Scripture passage is read, the person with that Chrismon will bring it forward, where it will be placed on the Chrismon Tree. The congregation will respond with its meaning.

Scripture Reading

The people who walked in darkness have seen a great light; those who dwelt in a land of deep darkness, on them has light shined. Thou hast multiplied the nation, thou hast increased its joy; they rejoice before thee as with joy at the harvest, as men rejoice when they divide the spoil. For the yoke of his burden, and the staff of his shoulder, the rod of his oppressor, thou hast broken as on the day of Midian. For every boot of the tramping warrior in battle tumult and every garment rolled in blood will be burned as fuel for the fire. For to us a child is born, to us a son is given; and the government will be upon his shoulder, and his name will be called Wonderful Counselor, Mighty God, Everlasting Father, Prince of Peace. Of the increase of his government and of peace there will be no end, upon the throne of David, and over his kingdom, to establish it, and to uphold it with justice and with righteousness from this time forth and for evermore. The zeal of the Lord of hosts will do this. (Isaiah 9:2-7)

Anthem of Nativity   "For Unto Us A Child Is Born" (Handel)
                                                         Contralto Soloist

Presentation of the Nativity Symbols

(The person with the appropriate Chrismon should bring it forward to the two decorators at the tree as the Scripture passage referring to that symbol is read.)

The Epiphany Star:
Now when Jesus was born in Bethlehem of Judea in the days of Herod the king, behold wise men from the East came to Jerusalem, saying, "Where is he who has been born King of the Jews? For we have seen his star in the East, and have come to worship him." (Matthew 2:1-2)
I am the root and the offspring of David, the bright morning star. (Revelation 22:16b)

(The Epiphany Star has five points and refers to the appearance and the revelation of Jesus as the Son of God. Peter speaks of the morning star rising in our hearts.)

People: **With hearts and soul we rejoice, for the Epiphany Star reminds us of God's morning star rising over our lives.**

The Christmas Rose:
The wilderness and the dry land shall be glad, the desert shall rejoice and blossom as the rose. It shall blossom abundantly, and rejoice even with joy and singing. (Isaiah 35:1-2a)

(This verse has been interpreted by some to be the Messianic Promise, and therefore the rose has come to represent Jesus, our Messiah. So the prophet proclaims the exultation of the redeemed.)

People: **With heart and soul we rejoice, for the Christmas Rose reminds us of God's love blossoming in our soul.**

The Manger:
In those days a decree went out from Caesar Augustus that all the world should be enrolled. This was the first enrollment, when Quirinius was governor of Syria. And all went to be enrolled, each to his own city. And Joseph also went up from Galilee, from the city of Nazareth, to Judea, to the city of David, which is called Bethlehem, because he was of the house and lineage of David, to be enrolled with Mary, his betrothed, who was with child. And while they were there, the time came for her to be delivered. And she gave birth to her first-born son and wrapped him in swaddling cloths, and laid him in a manger, because there was no place for them in the inn. (Luke 2:1-7)

People: **With heart and soul we rejoice, for the Manger reminds us of the humility with which God's son is born into our hearts.**

The Angel:
And in that region there were shepherds out in the field, keeping watch over their flock by night. And an angel of the Lord appeared to them, and the glory of the Lord shone around them, and they were filled with fear. And the angel said to them, "Be not afraid; for behold, I bring you good news of a great joy which will come to all the people; for to you is born this day in the city of David a Savior, who is Christ the Lord. And this will be a sign for you; you will find a babe wrapped in swaddling cloths and lying in a manger." And suddenly there was with the angel a multitude of the heavenly host praising God and saying, "Glory to God in the highest, and on earth peace among men with whom he is pleased." (Luke 2:8-14)

People: **With heart and soul we rejoice, for the Angel reminds us of heaven's joyous song over our coming salvation.**

Presentation of the Passion Symbols

It is right that we rejoice, that we honor him, that we sing his praise, for the glory of God is about him. Yet the love of God is greater than all the celestial splendor of the heavenly host. In that love, he gave up his life in innocent suffering. Like a lamb he was led to the slaughter, yet the powers of death could not contain that love. The powers of sin could not break that love. Now we know our Redeemer lives and has become the first fruits of them that sleep.

Anthem of Faith "I Know That My Redeemer Liveth" (Handel)
Soprano Solo

The Chalice:

Now as they were eating, Jesus took bread, and blessed, and broke it, and gave it to the disciples and said, "Take, eat; this is my body." And he took a cup, and when he had given thanks he gave it to them, saying, "Drink of it, all of you; for this is my blood of the new covenant which is poured out for many for the forgiveness of sins." (Matthew 26:26-28)

People: **With this offering we seek to honor him who took the cup of our suffering and drank of our sorrow, proclaiming the love of God.**

The Crosses

The Latin Cross:

Then Pilate handed him over to be crucified. So they took Jesus and he went out, bearing his own cross, to the place called in Hebrew, "Golgotha." There they crucified him and with him two others, one on either side, and Jesus between them. (John 19:16-18)

(This Cross with its longer upright than crossbar is the probable form on which Jesus was crucified; therefore, the foremost symbol of Christianity.)

The Jerusalem Cross:

The risen Christ said to Thomas, "Put your finger here, and see my hands; and put out your hand, and place it in my side: do not be faithless, but believing." (John 20:27)

(This Cross is in the form of a Greek cross with a smaller cross on each corner. The larger cross symbolizes the wounds in Christ's side and the smaller crosses, the wounds in his hands and feet.)

The Tau Cross with Serpent:

And as Moses lifted up the serpent in the wilderness, so must the Son of Man be lifted up, that whoever believes in him may have eternal life. (John 3:14-15)

(This symbol is a parallel between Christ's resurrection and an Old Testament story. When the Israelites were in the wilderness, many suffered death by being bitten by poisonous snakes. They begged Moses for relief, and God instructed Moses to make a serpent of brass and hang it on a pole. Anyone who was bitten by a snake was to look at the brass snake. When he did, he would live.)

People: **With this offering we seek to honor him who humbly laid down his power. In obedience he took up the Cross to conquer sin and death. We who were dead have seen and believed.**

The Sacrificial Lamb:

Surely he has borne our griefs and carried our sorrows; yet we esteemed him stricken, smitten by God, and afflicted. But he was wounded for our transgressions, he was bruised for our iniquities; upon him was the chastisement that made us whole, and with his stripes we are healed. All we like sheep have gone astray; we have turned every one to his own way; and the Lord has laid on him the iniquity of us all. He was oppressed, and he was afflicted, yet he opened not his mouth; like a lamb that is led to the slaughter, and like a sheep that before its shearers is dumb, so he opened not his mouth. (Isaiah 53:4-7)

The next day John the Baptist saw Jesus coming toward him and said, "Behold, the Lamb of God, who takes away the sin of the world! (John 1:29)

People: **With this offering we seek to honor him, for God has heard our cry and has answered our plea. God gave his son to die for us. O Lamb of God, grant us your peace.**

The Butterfly:

Now after the sabbath, toward the dawn of the first day of the week, Mary Magdalene and the other Mary went to see the sepulchre. And behold, there was a great earthquake; for an angel of the Lord descended from heaven and came and rolled back the stone, and sat upon it. His appearance was like lightning, and his raiment white as snow. And for fear of him the guards trembled and became like dead men. But the angel said to the women, "Do not be afraid; for I know that you seek Jesus who was crucified. He is not here, for he has risen as he said. Come, see the place where he lay. Then go quickly and tell his disciples that he has risen from the dead." (Matthew 28:1-7)

(Just as the caterpillar spins a cocoon and lies encased in a seemingly dead shell only to emerge in a changed form as a beautiful Butterfly, so Jesus was entombed, but rose from the dead.)

People: **With this offering we seek to honor him who burst forth triumphantly from the tomb. The same power that raised Jesus from the dead raises us out of our defeats and failures. His victory is our victory. Like the beautiful Butterfly, we emerge into the light of God's love.**

The Dove and Shell:
And when Jesus was baptized, he went up immediately from the water, and behold, the heavens were opened and he saw the Spirit of God descending like a dove, and alighting on him; and lo, a voice from heaven, saying, "This is my beloved Son, with whom I am well pleased." (Matthew 3:16-17)

The risen Christ instructed his disciples, "Go therefore and make disciples of all nations, baptizing them in the name of the Father and of the Son and of the Holy Spirit, teaching them to observe all that I have commanded you, and lo, I am with you always, to the close of the age." (Matthew 28:19-20)

(Just as Jesus was baptized at the beginning of his ministry, so the risen Christ instructed his disciples to go and baptize others. The Shell with three drops of water falling from it symbolizes baptism in the name of the Father, Son, and Holy Spirit.)

People: **With this offering we seek to honor him who baptizes us with the gift of salvation. With songs rejoicing we announce his coming. All glory, laud, and honor to you, our redeemer, king.**

Hymn of Honor   "All Glory, Laud, And Honor"

Presentation of the Symbols of Victory
In his victory over sin and death, Christ becomes our Redeemer and Savior. He, who could have conquered all in glory and power, chose instead to give himself in love. This is the joy which is to all people; that love was born at Christmas, love incarnate, love divine. May that love be yours, and may that love be mine. These last gifts we bring point to the VICTORIOUS CHRIST, who raises us up to be one with God.

The Chi Rho with Alpha and Omega:
He said to them, "But who do you say that I am?" Simon Peter replied, "You are the Christ, the Son of the living God." (Matthew 16:15-16)

(Chi and Rho are the first two letters of the Greek word "CHRISTOS," that is Christ. This is one of the most ancient of Christian symbols. The word, "Chrismon," when first used, specifically referred to the Chi-Rho of Christ's monogram.)

"I am the Alpha and the Omega, the first and the last, the beginning and the end." (Revelation 22:13)

(Alpha and Omega are the first and last letters of the Greek alphabet, and as such they symbolize Christ as the beginning and the end of all things.)

The Fish:
And he said to them, "Follow me, and I will make you fishers of men." (Matthew 4:19)

(The first letters of the Greek words for "Jesus Christ, God's Son, Savior" form the Greek word for fish, "ICTHUS.")

The Shepherd's Staff:
"I am the good shepherd. The good shepherd lays down his life for the sheep." (John 10:11)

(The Crook or Staff is the shepherd's tool for guiding his sheep, and therefore, symbolic of Christ, the Good Shepherd.)

The Cross and Orb:
In this the love of God was made manifest among us, that God sent his only Son into the world, so that we might live through him. In this is love, not that we loved God, but that he loved us and sent his Son to be the expiation for our sins. (1 John 4:9-10)

(The Orb or Sphere symbolizes the world and with a Cross, the triumph of Christ over it.)

The Iota-Chi:
Therefore God has highly exalted him and bestowed on him the name which is above every name, that at the name of Jesus every knee should bow, in heaven and on earth and under the earth, and every tongue confess that Jesus Christ is Lord, to the glory of God the Father. (Philippians 2:9-11)

(This Greek monogram consists of the first letters of the Greek words for "Jesus Christ.")

The Crown:
Then the seventh angel blew his trumpet, and there were loud voices in heaven, saying, "The kingdom of this world has become the Kingdom of our Lord and of his Christ, and he shall reign for ever and ever." (Revelation 11:15)

(The Crown symbolizes sovereignty and shows that Christ is the Ruler over all Creation.)

The Lamb with the Victory Banner:
After this I looked, and behold, a great multitude which no man could number, from every nation, from all tribes and peoples and tongues, standing before the throne and before the Lamb, clothed in white robes, with palm branches in their hands, and crying out with a loud voice, "Salvation belongs to our God who sits upon the throne, and to the Lamb!" And all the angels stood round the throne and round the elders and the four living creatures, and they fell on their faces before the throne and worshiped God, saying, "Amen! Blessing and glory and wisdom and thanksgiving and honor and power and might be to our God forever and ever. Amen." (Revelation 7:9-12)

The Circle with IHS:
"She will bear a son, and you shall call his name Jesus, for he will save his people from their sins." (Matthew 1:21)

(The Circle has been considered the perfect shape and symbolizes eternity, completeness, perfection. The Iota-Eta-Sigma monogram consists of the first three letters of the Greek word for "Jesus.")

Jesus Christ is the same yesterday and today and for ever. (Hebrews 13:8)

People: **Blessing and honor, wisdom and thanksgiving, glory and power, be unto him that sitteth upon the throne, and unto the lamb, forever and ever. Amen.**

Anthem of Victory   "The Hallelujah Chorus" (Handel)

Chrismon Prayer (in unison)
Almighty God, whose glory and majesty glows through the symbols of Christ, may these Chrismons ever remind us of your love entering our lives. May these gifts we have hung upon the tree become the gifts of your comfort and joy we share with others. So may we sing of redemption's happy dawn, for Jesus Christ is born in Bethlehem, through the heaven-born Prince of Peace, we pray. Amen.

Announcements

Hymn of Good Tidings and Joy   "God Rest You Merry Gentlemen"

Benediction and Choral Amen

Postlude   "Fanfare on Hark The Herald Angels Sing" (Wyton)

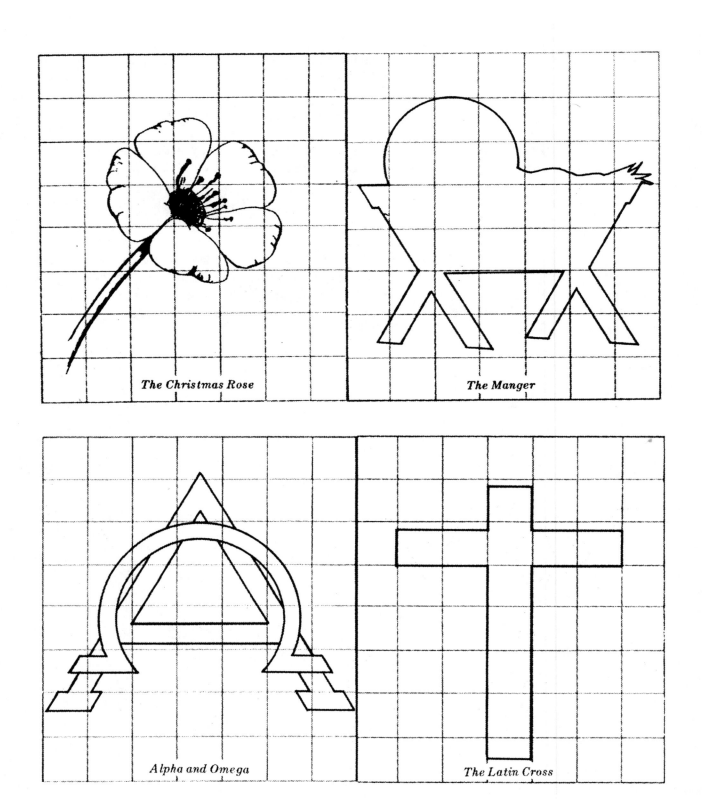

The Christmas Rose

The Manger

Alpha and Omega

The Latin Cross

34

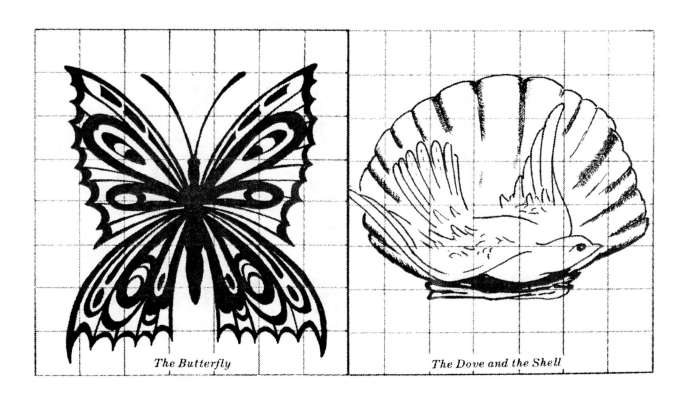

The Butterfly

The Dove and the Shell

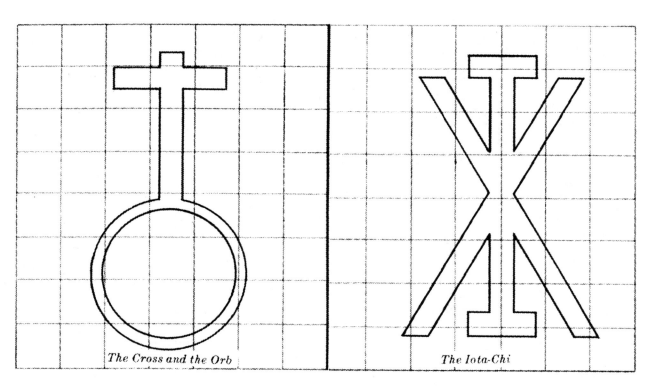

The Cross and the Orb

The Iota-Chi

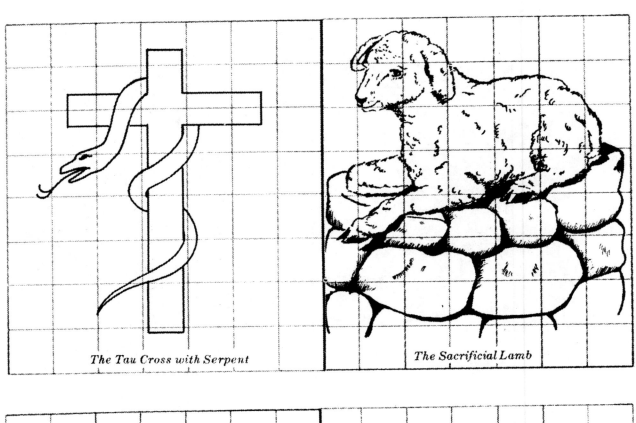

The Tau Cross with Serpent

The Sacrificial Lamb

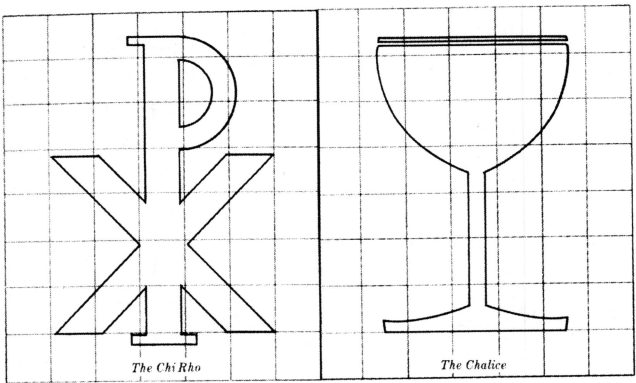

The Chi Rho

The Chalice

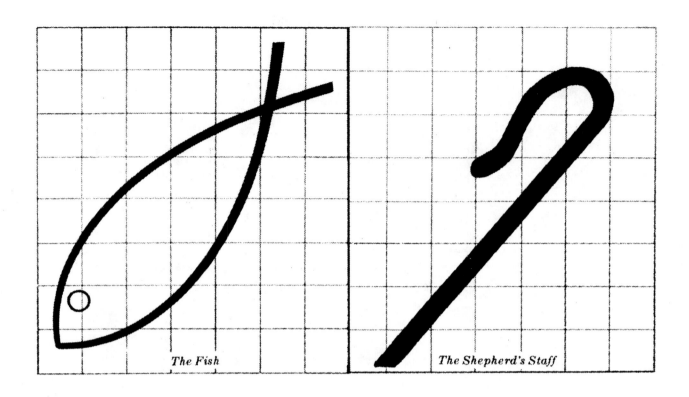

The Fish

The Shepherd's Staff

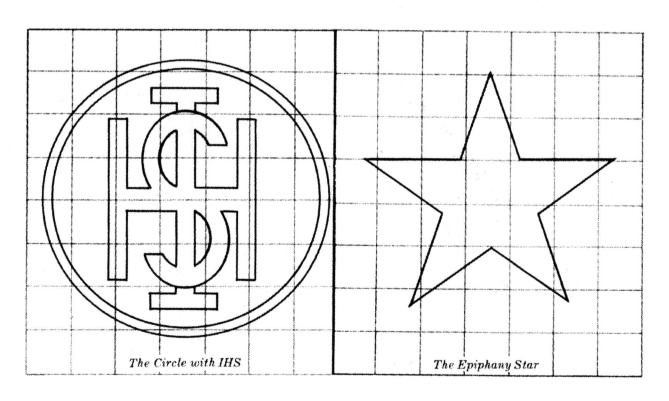

The Circle with IHS

The Epiphany Star

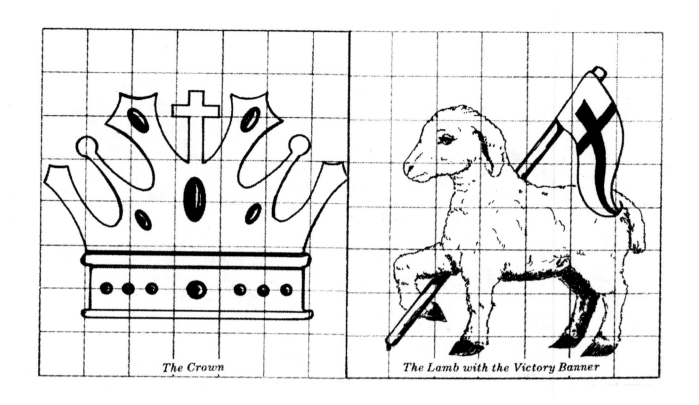

The Crown

The Lamb with the Victory Banner

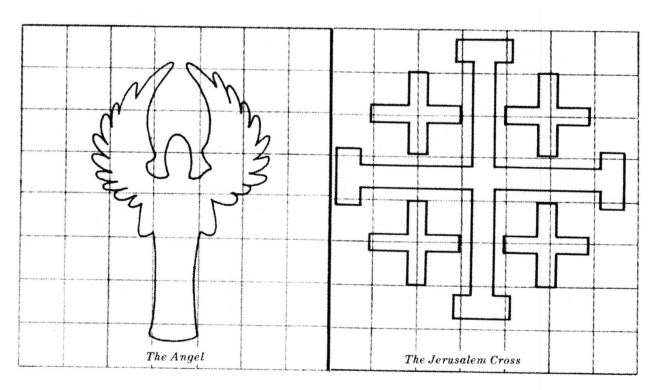

The Angel

The Jerusalem Cross

The
ABC's Of
Christmas

Four Easy Programs
For Christmas Worship Services

Elizabeth Morris-Pierce

Contents

The Angels Of Christmas

A Christmas Worship Service

The Prelude

The Words of Greeting

The Processional Hymn   "Hark! The Herald Angels Sing"
                                                            (Wesley/Mendelsohn)

(Here let both the church choir and the readers' choir process)

The Lighting of the Advent Wreath   (selected from John 1)
L: In the beginning was the Word, and the Word was with God, and the Word was God. *(light first candle)*
P: In him was life, and the life was the light of all people.
L: The light shines in the darkness, and the darkness has not overcome it. *(light second candle)*
P: That true light — that enlightens all persons — came into the world.
L: He was in the world, and the world was made through him, yet the world knew him not. *(light third candle)*
P: He came to his own home, and his own people received him not.
L: But to all who received him, who believed in his name, he gave power to become children of God. *(light fourth candle)*
P: And the Word became flesh and dwelt among us, full of grace and truth; we have beheld his glory, glory as of the only Son from the Father. *(light the Christ candle)*

The Congregational Prayer *(in unison)*
We bow before you in humble gratitude, Holy Lord, when we consider how you laid aside your glory to become one of us. You were divine and yet you became human in order to experience all that we mortals feel and endure. This is the glory of Christmas — the Word became flesh and dwelt among us. It is good that the angels sang of your glory, because your world failed to recognize you. Let us sense anew your presence, not only in the world, but in our own hearts. Our Emmanuel, make us pure and ready so that you may live within us, and by your grace, keep us pure until the day when we shall see you in the glory of your kingdom. Amen.

The Giving of our Gifts

The Offertory

The Congregational Response   "O Come, All Ye Faithful" (Adeste Fideles)

The Angels Of Christmas

The Visitation To Zechariah (based on Luke 1:15-20, 57-64)   Readers' Choir
The Anthem   "Let All Mortal Flesh Keep Silence" (French Carol Melody)
(may be sung as a canon)

The Visitation To Mary (based on Luke 1:26-38)   Readers' Choir
The Special Music   "Ave Maria" (J. S. Bach)
(vocal solo, or flute and piano)

The Visitation To Joseph (based on Matthew 1:18-25)   Readers' Choir
The Anthem   "Joseph, Joseph, Help Me Now" (German Carol)

The Visitation To The Shepherds (based on Luke 2:1-20)   Readers' Choir
The Anthem   (a "Gloria" of the choir's choice)
The Congregational Response   "Angels We Have Heard On High" (Traditional French Carol)

The Candlelighting Service
L: God sent heavenly messengers to announce the Incarnation. While we may not see the angels or hear their glorious anthem, our hearts can be attuned to their message.
P: Our hearts are ready to receive our Lord. We long to have him dwell within us so that we may follow his way.
L: Then I invite you to receive the Light of the World. From the Christ candle I will pass the light to you, and your mission is to pass the light to others.

The Candlelighting Hymn   "O Little Town Of Bethlehem" (Brooks/Redner)
(Sing verse 1; then on verse 2, begin passing the light as it is brought to you.)

The Benediction

The Hymn of Response   "Silent Night, Holy Night" (Stille Nacht)
(sing verses 1 and 4)

The Postlude

(All music selections are suggestions only. Other music may be used as desired.)

The Angels Of Christmas

Cast
>   Director of the Readers' Choir
>   Narrator (Male or Female)
>   Joseph (Deep Male Voice)
>   Angel Gabriel (Tenor Male Voice)
>   Mary (Female Voice)
>   The Readers' Choir, consisting of
>>   All Voices
>>   All Female Voices
>>   Young Female Voices
>>   Young Male Voices
>>   All Male Voices
>>   and miscellaneous solo voices as called for in the script

Suggestions

Let the Narrator stand at the lectern. The Readers' Choir should stand as a group for each of the four readings. It is effective if the Readers' Choir can be robed, along with the Singing Choir, or else let all wear the same color tops, skirts/pants.

The Readers' Choir should face the congregation so that the sound carries to the hearers.

Rehearsals are important to this presentation and should be done under the direction of a leader. Careful attention to diction, crescendos, breathing, and timing will add drama to the readings and offer the congregation a clear hearing of all the words. Do not hurry the readings, especially the solo voice parts.

The Visitation To Zechariah
For a Readers' Choir
based on Luke 1:5-20, 57-64

Narrator: Many, many years ago, when Herod was king of Judea, the duties of the priesthood were shared and the priests took turns to perform the various functions of the temple. There was a priest whose name was Zechariah, and Elizabeth was his wife.

Female Voices: Zechariah! Zechariah! A good man was he; righteous and obedient! Faithful and loyal was he to all the commandments and traditions of the Jewish faith.

Male Voices: And what of Elizabeth, that descendent of the High Priest, Aaron? Was she not also pure and blameless before God?

Young Female Voices: Yes, yes; she also was pure and blameless before God.

Narrator: But alas, Zechariah and Elizabeth had a sadness in their lives, for they had no children. As pure as Elizabeth may have been, others cast shame upon her for if she served God, why had God not given her a son?

Mature Female Voices: Poor Elizabeth! So pure and yet an outcast among her peers. And now it is too late, for she and her mate are old and beyond the years of childbearing. Poor Elizabeth!

Young Male Voices: Faithful Zechariah. Look! He must leave his dear wife to stay at the temple and tend the fires that burn the incense. Day and night the sweet-smelling incense rises to almighty Jehovah. The heavy fragrance rises like the prayers of the people who pray outside at the appointed hour.

All Voices: But where is Zechariah? Why does he remain so long in the temple? We smell the incense. Now let him come to us and speak words of comfort and assurance.

Narrator: While Zechariah was attending the altar of incense in the temple, the angel of the Lord suddenly stood there beside him. Zechariah was troubled at the sight.

Gabriel: "Do not fear, Zechariah. I have come to tell you that God has heard your prayers. Elizabeth will bear you a son, and you shall call his name John. He will be great before the Lord, and will turn many sons of Israel to their God. He will prepare the people for the coming of the Lord."

Narrator: Zechariah did not believe the words of the heavenly visitor and told the visage that he had come too late; he and Elizabeth were too old to bear a son.

Gabriel: "Do not doubt my words, Zechariah, for I am Gabriel and I am sent by God to bring this news to you. Because you doubt God's word, you will be unable to speak a word until all that I have spoken is fulfilled."

All Voices: Where is Zechariah? Where is Zechariah? Why does he not come and pray with us?

Female Voices: Zechariah, why are you silent? Please pray with us.

Narrator: But Zechariah was speechless, and he remained speechless until after the birth of his son.

Female Voices: Congratulations, Elizabeth, congratulations! After which ancestor will you name your son?

Female Voice: Our son will blaze new paths; no ancestor's name for him. He will be named John.

All Voices: No, no, Elizabeth. You are wrong. Tell us, Zechariah, after which member of the family will you name your son?

Narrator: Zechariah was still without voice, so he motioned for a writing tablet and wrote: "His name is John." Immediately he was able to speak.

All Voices: Jehovah be praised! Surely the son of Zechariah and Elizabeth will be great among our people. We have witnessed a miracle.

Suggested Anthem: "Let All Mortal Flesh Keep Silence" (French Carol Melody)

The Visitation To Mary
For a Reader's Choir
based on Luke 1:26-38

Mature Female Voices: Mary is a good girl, a good daughter, a joy to her family.

Solo Female Voice 1: She helped raise her siblings.

Solo Female Voice 2: She cleans the house and keeps the water jars filled.

Solo Female Voice 3: She bakes fine bread and tends the garden.

Male Voices: Mary will make a fine wife. Fortunate the man to whom she is given in marriage.

Joseph: Yes, fortunate the man who will marry Mary of Nazareth. Be envious of me, for I am the one to whom this sweet maiden has been given.

Male Voices: You are fortunate, indeed! For Mary is devoted to God and to her family. She will make a good wife.

Narrator: And so it was arranged by Mary's family that she was to become the wife of Joseph when she came of age. The betrothal was announced and the village rejoiced at the news, for they all knew of the goodness of Mary.

Young Female Voices: God in heaven also knew of the goodness of Mary, and she found favor with the Almighty.

Older Female Voices: Why can't all the young women of the village be like Mary?

Young Female Voices: We don't have time for so much devotion; we enjoy life and have fun.

Male Voices: Yes, that is true. Few there be like Mary.

Narrator: One day, while Mary was alone in her room, she was surprised by a visitor whose appearance was unlike any she had ever seen.

Gabriel: "Greetings to you, favored one. The Lord is with you!"

Mary: Who is this person? Why does he say the Lord *is* with me? How does he know this? And how did he get here?

Narrator: Such were the thoughts that troubled Mary at the appearance of the strange visitor as he greeted her.

Gabriel: Please do not be afraid, Mary. You, of all women, have found favor with the Almighty God. God has chosen you to bear a son, a very special son, whose name shall be called Jesus.

Narrator: Now Mary's thoughts became more troubled than ever. She was dumbfounded; unable to speak. The visitor continued ...

Gabriel: I am Gabriel, Mary, and I was sent by God to tell you that you will give birth to a son. He will be great, and he will be called the Son of the Most High.

Solo Male Voice: The Lord God will give to him the throne of his father David, and he will reign over the house of Jacob forever; and of his kingdom there will be no end.

Narrator: At last, Mary's voice found its tongue.

Mary: How can this be, since I have no husband?

Female Voices: Yes, how can this be? Children must not be conceived outside the bonds of marriage.

Gabriel: I know that you are not married, but the Holy Spirit will come upon you and the power of the Most High will overshadow you. The child you bear will be holy, it will be the Son of God!

Solo Female Voice: Every Jewish woman through the centuries has longed to be the mother of the Messiah, but none of us was found worthy.

Solo Male Voice: Only Mary found favor with God.

Narrator: The angel, Gabriel, told Mary about her cousin Elizabeth's miracle pregnancy, saying:

All Voices: For with God, nothing is impossible!

Mary: Behold, kind sir, I am devoted to my God and I will obediently submit myself to bearing the Son of God. Let it be to me according to your word.

All Voices: And Mary's soul magnified the Lord and her spirit rejoiced in God because he had regard for her, and now all generations called her blessed.

Suggested Musical Selection: "Ave Maria" (J. S. Bach)

The Visitation To Joseph
For a Readers' Choir
based on Matthew 1:18-25

Narrator: While Mary had found favor with God, and while the child that grew in her womb was the holy Son of God, this was a secret Mary held deep within her own heart.

Female Voices: What a rascal, that Joseph. Could he not wait until the marriage was consummated?

Solo Male Voice: You said that Mary was pure and devoted to God. How could such a thing happen?

Female Voices: But she is engaged to be married to Joseph. Surely everyone will understand and accept this situation of her pregnancy.

Joseph: Perhaps others can accept this situation, but I cannot. The child which my fiancée bears is not mine. I cannot bear this shame and embarrassment.

Narrator: Joseph had the legal and religious right to bring Mary to trial. If the child was not his, he had the right to have her punished — even put to death.

Male Voices: Tell us, Joseph, what will you do?

Solo Male Voice 1: Will you seek revenge from this faithless girl?

Solo Male Voice 2: Will you drag her before the authorities?

Female Voices: Yes, yes! Make her pay for her infidelity. Show no mercy.

Joseph: She is so young, so innocent. Whatever happened to her was not her fault, I am certain of it. I cannot bring her before the authorities; she endures enough shame.

All Voices: Ah, Joseph, you are a good man, a fine man. It is Mary who is fortunate to be betrothed to you.

Narrator: Joseph was indeed a fine and good man. Rather than cause Mary future shame, he decided that he would break their engagement quietly.

All Voices: Break the engagement to Mary?

Narrator: In those days that was the same as obtaining a writ of divorce.

All Voices: Poor Mary! Poor Joseph! Poor little baby that would be born without a father!

Narrator: So while Joseph was trying to find a way to divorce his fiancée discreetly, he fell into a troubled sleep, and lo, an angel of the Lord appeared to him in a dream.

Gabriel: Joseph! Joseph! Listen to me, Joseph. God has sent me to you to tell you the truth.

All Male Voices: Joseph, descendent of King David, you have been chosen by God to be a father to Mary's son. Do not fear to take Mary to be your wife.

All Voices: That which is conceived in her is of the Holy Spirit — Mary has done no wrong.

Gabriel: She will bear a son and you will call his name Jesus. Mary's son will save his people from their sins.

Female Voices: Do not divorce Mary, Joseph. Accept what has happened and enfold her to your breast. Comfort her and tell her that you understand.

All Voices: From God's own messenger you have heard it: Mary is a good and pure woman. Help her through this crisis. Share both her shame and her glory.

Male Voices: Behold! A virgin shall conceive and bear a son, and his name shall be called Emmanuel.

All Voices: Emmanuel — God with us!

Narrator: When Joseph woke from his sleep, he did as the angel of the Lord commanded him; he took Mary for his wife, but knew her not until she had borne a son; and he called his name Jesus.

Suggested Anthem: "Joseph, Joseph Help Me Now" (German Carol)

The Visitation To The Shepherds
For a Readers' Choir
based on Luke 2:1-20

Narrator: In those days a decree went out from Caesar Augustus declaring that all people in lands conquered by Rome must be counted. This census was the first — when Quirinius was governor of Syria.

All Voices: Everyone was required to return to their city of ancestry in order to be enrolled for the census.

Male Voices: Because Joseph was a descendent of King David, he left the city of Nazareth, and traveled to the city of David, which is called Bethlehem.

Solo Female Voice: Did he travel alone?

Male Voices: No, he and Mary went together to the city of Bethlehem.

Female Voices: Bethlehem is a four-day trek from Nazareth. Why did Joseph take a pregnant girl on such an arduous journey?

Narrator: The time for delivery was nearly here. Joseph could not leave his wife alone at such a crucial time.

Solo Female Voice: Besides, they trusted in God. It was God's Son she was bearing and God would take care of them.

Narrator: Yes, and while they were in Bethlehem, she gave birth to her firstborn son.

Female Voices: She wrapped him in swaddling cloths and laid him in a manger — a feeding trough for animals.

Male Voices: What else could they do? There was no room in all of Bethlehem because of the Great Enrollment.

All Voices: No room! No room for the Son of God, so she laid him in a manger.

Female Voices: That means the Son of God was born in a stable?

Male Voices: To be more exact, the Son of God was born in a cave, for just beyond Bethlehem were the many caves which farmers and shepherds used to house their animals.

Solo Female Voice: Mary and Joseph trusted God and did not complain that they had no comfortable room at the inn in which they could stay. They made the best of the situation.

Male Voices: At least the tiny Son of God was warmed by the presence of the animals in the stable, and he could sleep on soft hay.

Female Voices: But think of the stench! Think of the filth!

Male Voices: Remember that Joseph was a good man and that he probably did what he could to make the area as clean as possible for the birth of God's Son.

All Voices: You are right. They were prepared for the birth of Jesus, even to bring the special swaddling cloths to wrap his tiny body.

Narrator: It was the spring of the year and the shepherds were in the fields, allowing their sheep to graze on the new grass rather than keep them penned up for the night.

Male Voices: Behold how dark the night! It is good that the wool of the sheep is white, or we would not be able to see them in this blackness.

Younger Male Voices: It is cold tonight. Not even the fire keeps us warm.

Male Voices: Make the fire larger. Let us brighten the night and get warm.

Narrator: Even as they spoke, the night became suddenly brighter and they knew not why.

Solo Male Voice 1: What is that glow?

Solo Male Voice 2: It is the fire.

Solo Male Voice 3: No, no, my friends. It is not the fire! Turn around and see what I see.

Male Voices: There *is* a great light, and a man stands in the midst of it!

Solo Male Voice 1: How did he get here?

Solo Male Voice 2: What magic is this?

Gabriel: This is no magic that you see. I am an angel of the Lord God Almighty.

Male Voices: An angel? Appearing to us? How do we merit such honor?

Gabriel: No one else will listen. The city is too busy; the people are too busy. God has chosen you to receive the good news.

Male Voices: What news? Tell us the good news!

Gabriel: The happy news which I share with you is for *all* people, but you hear it first. On this very night, in the city of David, a Savior has been born — for you and all persons. The child is the Lord! The Messiah! The long-awaited Messiah!

Male Voices: We are only dirty shepherds, yet you have come to us from God to tell us this good news!

Gabriel: Wait, there's more. So that you know that all I have said is true, go to Bethlehem and see for yourselves. In a stable you will find the holy babe. He is lying in a manger, all wrapped in swaddling cloths.

Narrator: Before the shepherds could respond to the heavenly messenger, they were suddenly surrounded with a multitude of the heavenly beings whose voices rose in a glorious anthem:

All Voices: Glory to God in the highest, glory to God in the highest! And on earth, peace among men with whom God is pleased!

Narrator: The song echoed and rang from hillside to hillside. Never had the shepherds witnessed the glory of God before. At last the light faded and the song drifted slowly away.

Male Voices: My brothers, let us find out for ourselves. The angel of the Lord said to look for a baby lying in a manger.

Young Male Voice: But there are many, many caves near Bethlehem.

Older Male Voice: Then we shall search every one until we find the Messiah! Come, let us go find him.

Narrator: And they went with haste to find the Savior.

Mary: Joseph, what do I hear? Listen, someone approaches.

Joseph: It is a group of shepherds, Mary. They have come for warmth, no doubt. Welcome, friends, come in and be warm.

Male Voices: Thank you, kind sir, but we have come to find the Messiah. We have searched many animal shelters to find him of whom the angels sing.

Joseph: Then it is my pleasure to tell you that your search has ended. Come. See where he lays.

Male Voices: It is as the angel told us. The babe is wrapped in swaddling cloths and lies in a manger.

All Voices: Ahhhhh. See the little baby. Hushhhhh. The Savior of the world is sleeping. Let us worship the newborn king and pay him our homage.

Narrator: And when the shepherds saw that what the angels had said had come true, they told everyone they met of the good news concerning the child. However, those who heard them wondered at what the shepherds said and wondered why they sang all the way as they returned to their fields.

All Voices: As for Mary, the mother of the holy child, she held on to all that happened, and pondered on them in her heart.

Narrator: Now, good people, you have heard the stories of how the angels of God visited earth to bring good news of redemption and peace to all. You have heard the story of God's Incarnation!

Suggested Music: a "Gloria" of the choir's choice

(Here let the Christmas Worship Service continue)

The Bells Of Christmas

A Christmas Eve Worship Service

The Prelude

The Welcome

The Carol   "O Come, All Ye Faithful"

The Lighting of the Advent Wreath
(Leader rings a bell — either a handbell or some other small bell. Candlelighters are young people wearing jingle bells around their ankles)

Leader: Come forth, merry candlelighters. It is time to brighten our chancel with the warmth of candlelight. Come and reawaken the candles that once glowed during the season of Advent.

Candlelighter 1:   I bring a flame to the candles of Hope and Joy, for tonight our hope is fulfilled in the joy of this holy festival.

Candlelighter 2:   Then let me bring light to the candles of Love and Peace, for tonight we celebrate the birth of the Prince of Peace and the King of Love.

Candlelighter 3:   The candle that I light is pure and white because it represents the pure Son of God whose birthday we celebrate.

Leader: Well done, merry candlelighters. Now you may join the worshipers and together we will offer our prayer of thanksgiving.

The Congregational Prayer *(in unison)*
Holy and gracious God, we come with grateful and happy hearts because you remembered your creation and provided for us so great a salvation. Because of Jesus, we can know peace and forgiveness from sin; we can experience love and joy because you first loved us. Grant that we shall walk in the light of this sacred night and carry it to a world that longs to know a better way — the way of your Son, our Lord, Christ Jesus. Amen.

The First Scripture Reading   John 1:1-5, 10-11

The Carol   "Good Christian Men, Rejoice" (congregation)

The First Bell of Christmas
(Reader rings a bell) Tonight we rejoice in the good news of Christmas, but 2,000 years ago there were no bells ringing and only a few were privileged to hear the song of the angels. Just a handful of people were prepared to receive God's incarnation; the rest of the world sat in a stupor of worn-out hope that had become more of a habit than a vital faith. Quietly the Source of Life brought

light to the world, but eyes were looking for a more spectacular light. To this day, eyes look to the dazzling lights of neon and the silver screen, and we miss the gentle glow of God's love and acceptance.

The Second Scripture Reading   Luke 1:68-69, 78-79

The Carol   "I Heard The Bells On Christmas Day"
(May be either a choral anthem or handbell choir anthem)

The Second Bell of Christmas
(Reader vigorously rings sleigh/jingle bells) Christmas was not always a joyful celebration. Our Puritan Forefathers punished those who participated in outward celebrations. But those who have experienced the true joy of Christ's coming cannot hide it inside for long; such joy must be shared. Let us take the good news to our neighbors. Harness the horses to the sleigh and let the sleigh bells ring! Don't keep your joy hidden within. Share it with others. Ring the bells and sing the carols of Christmas!

The Third Scripture Reading   Luke 2:1-7

The Carol   "Away In A Manger"
(May be a choral anthem, or presented by a children's choir)

The Fourth Scripture Reading   Luke 2:8-20

The Third Bell of Christmas
(Reader rings a very large handbell — or else someone may ring the bell in the church steeple) Christmas has many symbols: Santa Claus, snowmen, reindeer, candy canes, Christmas trees, candles, holly sprigs ... and bells. Bells were used to attract attention to an important announcement. The old Town Crier rang his bell as he called the news up and down the streets. When a bell sounded in the classroom, it was usually followed by a message from the principal's office. Church bells call us to worship, and on this night of nights we are called to observe the celebration of the birth of Christ Jesus.

Only the shepherds heard the song of the angels the night Jesus was born. How I wish that every bell in every tower and steeple could ring out — all at once — to proclaim the glorious news that God sent us a Savior, and his name is Jesus! I wonder if people all over the world would come to worship him?

The Fifth Scripture Reading   John 13:3-5, 34-35

The Carol   "Love Came Down At Christmas"
(May be either a handbell anthem or choral anthem)

The Fourth Bell of Christmas
(Reader rings a small bell) This bell reminds me of the bells I hear ringing from every street corner each Christmas season; it reminds me of the bells which are rung by the volunteers at the Salvation

Army Christmas kettles. All day long, from Thanksgiving until Christmas, they ring that little bell, hoping people will be reminded to stop and share so that the needy may have a brighter holiday.

Christians are people who follow the Way of Christ. They really should not need to hear little bells ringing to remind them to share love and resources. First God shared with us by sending his Son. Then Jesus set us an example of how to live and love. There are bells that we can ring as we try to follow his example. We can let the telephone bells ring when we call others and invite them to worship. We can let the doorbells ring when we call upon the sick and the lonely. We can let the jingle bells of good will ring when we brighten the lives of the needy.

These are all the bells of Christmas, bells ringing out the glorious song of the angels: Christ is born!

The Christmas Meditation (Pastor)

The Candlelighting Service
L: The tradition of the Christmas Eve Candlelighting Ceremony brings to us in a very real way the great effect of sharing. While we sing this favorite carol of Christmas, our sanctuary will be darkened, except for the light of the Advent Wreath. From the Christ candle I will share the light of Christ with you, and you, in turn will share your light with your neighbor, until this darkened room becomes aglow with the soft, gentle light that comes from each person.

The Carol   "Silent Night, Holy Night"

The Benediction

The Postlude

Ideas For Presentation

If your church has a handbell choir, this service provides a way to feature this group by having them play some of the carols listed in the program.

However, not all churches are fortunate enough to have a handbell choir, and this service may be presented equally as effectively with the use of miscellaneous bells and/or using the carillon stop on the church organ.

Also, the carols may be sung by a soloist or the congregation if your church does not have a choir.

The Colors Of Christmas

Ideas For This Presentation

This program is designed for presentation by a church choir and eight readers as part of a Christmas Eve Worship Service. However, it can also be used by churches without a choir by having the congregation sing the Christmas carols as listed with each reading.

A table should be placed in the chancel area and covered with a white cloth. On it place eight candles to match the colors of the readings. Long six-inch-wide strips of colored cloth should be rolled up at the base of each candle holder, each strip matching the color of the candle. As the readings are presented, an acolyte (or the reader) lights the candle and unrolls the colored cloth so that it drapes down over the edge of the table, as pictured in the illustration below.

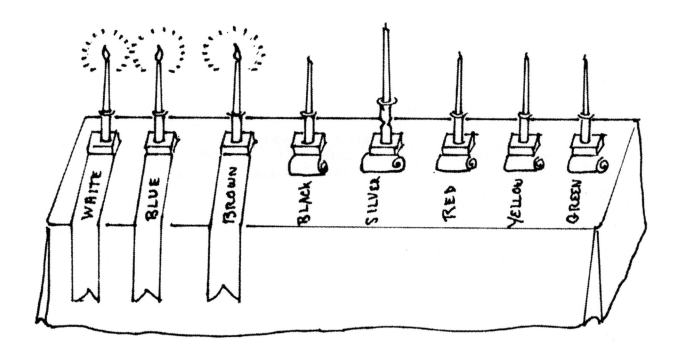

The Colors Of Christmas

A Christmas Eve Worship Service

The Prelude

The Welcome

The Carol   "Joy To The World"

The Lighting of the Advent Wreath
L: The lights of Hope, Joy, Love, and Peace have warmed our hearts while we prepared for the coming of the Christ during the past four weeks of Advent.
P: We long for the coming of God's Son into our lives.
L: Be of good cheer for tonight we honor the birth of Jesus, the Christ, the Son of God, in whose honor we light the center candle in our Advent Wreath.
P: O come to us; abide with us, dear Jesus, that the lights of Hope, Joy, Love, and Peace may never be extinguished.

The Congregational Prayer *(in unison)*
We bow before you, Almighty God, to thank you for your gift of light in a dark world of sin. Thank you for sending us a Savior. We come to thank you for this holy gift, and as we offer our gratitude, we also offer ourselves. Cast out our sin and enter into our hearts. Be born in us so we may be worthy followers of Jesus, who came to show us the way to live, and in whose name we pray. Amen.

The Christmas Scripture Reading   Luke 2:1-20

The Colors Of Christmas

1. White
(White candle is lighted and the white banner unrolled. Choir hums: "Angels We Have Heard On High" during reading)

 White, very white, was the color of the angel's robe, and gentle his mission this holy day; for he was the very first herald of the Messiah. Soft was the light in the room as he spoke to a Jewish maiden: "I bring you greetings from the Most High! For you are highly favored among all women. In due time you shall conceive, and the child that shall be born of you is to be the Savior of the world; and you shall call his name Jesus."

 I light this first candle of the Christmas Story with a prayer that the purity of white will never be stained by the deeds of humankind.

(Choir sings verse 1 and refrain of "Angels We Have Heard On High")

White is the color of snow — fresh, beautiful snow that covers ugliness with fluffy white. White is the color of the lambs in our manger scenes, reminding us that the Christmas Baby became the Lamb of God who took away the sins of the world. Jesus is the perfect, pure white Lamb of God.

2. Blue

(Blue candle is lighted and blue banner unrolled as soloist sings "Ave Maria" — or it may be played as an instrumental solo before reader tells of the color blue)

Blue was the sky that very special day, as blue as the soft shawl draped around the maiden's shoulders. And if loyalty is the color of blue, it must be because of Mary's faithfulness to the high charge presented to her by the heavenly visitor. Silently she endured the shame until the time of her marriage; and silently she accepted the strange and difficult life she must now live; for her mother-heart would know extreme pain and grief.

Let the light of this blue candle stir us to a loyalty so that the world may see the "true blue" of Christianity.

3. Brown

(Choir sings verses 1-4 and 6 of "The Friendly Beasts" as the brown candle is lighted and the brown banner unrolled)

Brown is the color of the beasts of burden, the animals who warmed the stable where Jesus lay. Brown is the color of the humble people, the diligent, working-class of people. Brown was the color of the robe which Joseph wore. Joseph was committed to his employment as a carpenter; Joseph was committed to his love for his young bride. He did not understand all the things of which the angel spoke; but Joseph did not question, he placed his trust in Jehovah.

The color of this candle is not dull; brown is as vital as the living earth; as vibrant as the cedars of Lebanon which Joseph would carve into a useful product. Therefore, let this candle remind us of the vitality of everyday life. Let Christmas live in our everyday activities.

4. Black

(Choir sings verse 1 of "O Come, O Come, Emmanuel" — no refrain, while black candle is lighted and black banner unrolled)

The age was black, as black as any age had ever been; as black as the deeds of the people who lived in that age. God's chosen people were captive; their spirits broken in all areas, save one: their religion. The mighty Romans were powerless against the unbroken faith of the Jewish people in an omnipotent God.

Although the people were submissive in matters of religion, there was no choice but to submit to Caesar and his decree of taxation. All, including Mary and Joseph, must travel to the city of their birth to be registered for the census. It mattered not that Mary was soon to have her child; she must travel on foot the same as Joseph and all other Jews in captivity.

Yet, no matter how dark the age, the candle glows even brighter when we hear the words: "In the fullness of time, God sent His Son to be the Savior."

(Choir bursts forth with refrain: "Rejoice, Rejoice" of "O Come, O Come, Emmanuel")

5. Silver

(This reader lights the silver candle, which should be higher than the others, and unfolds the silver banner, which can be silver lamé)

The black cloud has a silver lining, we are told. Into the very blackest night came the silver ray of Hope. For in Bethlehem, the city of Mary and Joseph's sojourn, the baby Jesus was born.

His parents were prepared for his coming: they had the swaddling bands ready and they knew just what to do.

But Bethlehem was not prepared for the coming of the Lord. So crowded was the city because of the census, the lowly couple could only find shelter in a stable. There the child would be kept warm by the animals, and his cradle would be a soft bed of hay.

It must have been difficult to see the silver amidst the black of hardships in that dark and pungent stable. But Mary knew God must have a purpose, so she chose not to complain.

As the silver Christ candle glows, we wish with all our hearts that its light would outshine all others so that the world may see and believe!

6. Red

(Choir male voices sing verse 1 of "What Child Is This" and female voices join in on the refrain, while the red candle is lighted and red banner unrolled)

Red, as red as drops of blood, were the berries nestled among the green bushes on the hillside. And grazing among the bushes were sheep as shepherds casually watched over their flocks.

It was night time, it was cold, and lonely, and even dull; but not for long. For the shepherds heard and saw a sight that few others have been privileged to hear or see. The sound was glorious! Like a thousand angels singing all around them.

(Choir sings refrain of "Angels We Have Heard On High")

And then a voice told them the reason for all this joy. "Go into Bethlehem, and there, lying in a feeding trough filled with hay, you will find a tiny newborn baby. Go, worship him, for this child is God's Messiah — the Christ."

Then the thousands of angels broke into the refrain: "Glory to God in the Highest, and on earth, peace to persons of good will."

At last! God's Messiah had come! The shepherds hurried away to find the baby and worship him, and as they went on their way, one shepherd reached out and picked the green branches of the bush that was covered with the blood-red berries, that he might present it to the infant Jesus.

(Men sing verse 3 of "What Child Is This" and women join in on the refrain)

7. Yellow

(The yellow candle is lighted and the yellow banner rolled out)

The black age was pierced by still another light — the yellow light of the star. There were, in another country, some learned men who studied very closely the star patterns in the sky. Their excitement rose to a peak when one night they viewed a super nova, and they reasoned among themselves that this must surely be a sign!

In their studies they came across an ancient prophecy which foretold the birth of a mighty king; a king who would alter the philosophy of humankind forever. And so, they followed the yellow glimmer of this mighty star; bearing kingly gifts for the royal infant; gold, myrrh, and frankincense.

We, too, as we gaze at the light of this yellow candle, desire to bring the Christ Child a royal gift. We can do more. We can give him what we are; we can give him our hearts.
(Full choir sings verse 3 of "In The Bleak Mid-Winter")

8. Green
(The green candle is lighted and the green banner rolled out)

One more color is very necessary to our Christmas Story: the color of the eternal hills; the color of holly; the color of the never-ending fir tree; the color of green.

"O God, our help in ages past; our hope for years to come ..." and still the years go by, and still the ages appear black or even worse — a dull, shabby gray. Must eternity roll by before the peace of Christmas becomes a living reality? Did the Christ Child live and die without a reason?

NO! Because the Christmas Story ends in resurrection! Even before the snow has gone, the green shoots appear, bursting forth with new life, as we behold resurrection every spring. This Christmas candle of green is a permanent reminder that the Christ Child still lives, and that he can live in our hearts.
(Choir sings verses 3 and 4 of "Oh, Little Town Of Bethlehem")

The Pastoral Prayer

The Lord's Prayer *(in unison)*

The Candlelighting Carol   "Silent Night, Holy Night"

The Candlelighting Service
(The lights in the sanctuary should be extinguished)

Leader: Let the darkness of the sanctuary be symbolic of the darkness of the world. Into the dark world the Light has come, and as I take the light from the Christ candle and offer it to you, so may you take the Light and offer it to others. Bring your tapers to the light of the candles held by the ushers, and continue to sing (or hum) the carol until all the candles are lighted and the sanctuary glows with the light of Christmas. Then, let us be silent as we gaze in awe upon the light, that we may reflect on how great a light was begun with one tiny flame.

The Benediction

The Postlude

The Gifts Of Christmas

Ideas For This Presentation

Seven persons should be chosen to make the gift presentations. Use either the altar or a special table draped with a cloth as the Worship Center on which is placed two candelabra. The pyramid (or "tree") of gifts will be built up between the candelabra, as pictured in the below illustration,

Large boxes of facial tissue — wrapped in bright green gift wrap, are ideal for the first two rows of the pyramid. The top two rows could be the boutique-size tissue boxes wrapped as gifts. Each gift should be clearly labeled. The top gift of "Love" can either be in the form of a star or else it can have a star attached to it to complete the pyramid/tree.

The "Gift" presenter comes forward to read his or her part and then places the "Gift" on the Worship Center. As each "Gift" is presented, let an acolyte light a candle on each of the candelabra.

The Gifts Of Christmas

A Christmas Eve Worship Service

The Prelude

The Welcome

The Lighting of the Advent Wreath

L: Christ candle, symbol of Light come to earth; symbol of purity and goodness; we light you as we celebrate the birthday of our King, Jesus.

P: From your brilliance we receive the flame which shall light the candles of Hope, Love, and Joy, which grace our Advent wreath.

L: There is yet one candle remaining to be lit; the symbol for Peace.

P: Peace candle, as you receive your light from the Christ candle, so may we be aware of the peace which we receive from the Christ.

L: Jesus said: "My peace I give to you ... such as the world cannot give."

The Congregational Prayer *(in unison)*

Lord Jesus, you are the Source of light; you are the Prince of Peace. The world needs the peace you offer. We pray that these symbols of Advent which have been set ablaze this night, will remind us that we are to help spread your love and peace throughout the world. Amen.

The Introduction (Pastor)

Tonight we celebrate the birthday of the King. His realm is the kingdom of peace and truth. His coronation will take place when his kingdom makes its final triumph over evil and injustice. But today we honor his birth. What shall we bring him on his birthday?

> *What can I give him, poor as I am?*
> *If I were a shepherd, I would bring a lamb;*
> *if I were a Wise Man, I would do my part;*
> *yet what can I give him: give my heart.*
> (C. Rossetti)

On this Christmas Eve we will lay our gifts before him, offering them in humility as we celebrate the birth of Jesus, our Emmanuel. Amen.

The Gift of Hope

Scripture   Isaiah 7:14; 40:3-5, 11

Presentation of the Gift of Hope

I bring the gift of Hope, because Christmas began with the promise of hope. Each year at Advent we wait; we hope; we anticipate the fulfillment of God's promise to send a Savior to the world.

We wait for phone calls, for Christmas cards, for invitations to parties, for wonderful meals, for guests, and for Santa to arrive. Sometimes, in the quiet moments of meditation, I think of people who have different hopes than these:

- the poor families who hope someone will remember their needs;
- the prisoner who hopes to be released and start a new life;
- the hospital patients who hope for healing;
- the refugee mother who hopes to find her children;
- the nursing home resident who hopes that someone will visit; and
- the homeless who hope for a place of shelter from the cold.

This night we will celebrate our Hope fulfilled as we hail the birth of the promised Messiah. As I present this gift, I recognize that Jesus placed Hope in his followers to carry the promise of salvation and a new kingdom to the whole earth. My gift to him is to do my part to bring hope to others.

The Carol   "There's A Song In The Air"

The Gift of Faith

Scripture   Luke 1:26-38

Presentation of the Gift of Faith

Like all devout Jews, Mary and her family had hope concerning the coming Messiah. Of Mary, however, deep faith was required if she was to believe the angelic vision. Hers was no surface faith. With remarkable courage she lived and acted in belief and obedience to God's will.

In honor of Mary, the mother of our Lord, I present this gift of Faith:

- To be pregnant with the Son of God, and unmarried, required faith and inner strength.
- To undertake a long journey by foot in her final trimester of pregnancy, required faith and courage.
- To bring a child into the world in the crude setting of an animal shelter required faith and humility.
- To experience the unusual events of angelic visions, shepherds' visits, and Magi's gifts, required faith that kept her going even though she did not completely comprehend.

I, too, would be a faithful servant of the Most High.

The Anthem (by the choir or special music)

The Gift of Peace

Scripture   Luke 2:8-14

Presentation of the Gift of Peace

God gave to us the Prince of Peace. The angels promised peace to people of good will. As I present this Gift of Peace, I have this feeling within me that the peace of which the angels sang in Bethlehem is not a "laying down of swords" kind of peace. Rather it is a spiritual calm that comes into the lives of those who accept and believe in the Prince of Peace.

When all persons finally learn this peace, and not until then, will global peace become a reality. Then perhaps Isaiah's vision of peace will finally happen. No one shall cause hurt in all God's kingdom.

Little Prince of Peace, instill your peace within our hearts, today as I offer my gift of my promise to become a peace-maker.

The Carol   "O, Little Town Of Bethlehem"

The Gift of Friends and Family

Scripture   Genesis 2:18, 21-24; Matthew 1:18-25

Presentation of the Gift of Friends and Family

Christmas is Family: The get-to-gethering around the Christmas tree and in the dining room; the giving and receiving of gifts; the laughter and tears of the children; the sharing of stories between the adults; the solidarity of relatives who support one another.

Christmas is Friends, both near and afar; as they send cards, keep in touch, and renew old memories.

But will we remember those who are lonely — or in nursing homes and hospitals? Will we remember with compassion the friends and families who are grieving this Christmas?

I present the Gift of Friends and Family with the realization that not everyone will be happy this Christmas, and with a prayer that the peace and gentleness of this season will help heal their pain and sorrow.

The Congregational Prayer

L: The Lord be with you.

P: And also with you.

L: Let us pray together:

All: Father God, giver of the most perfect gift of all, we bow before you this Christmas Eve with hearts full of adoration. Grant your forgiveness, we pray and make us worthy to receive the pure and holy Savior into our hearts and lives. May we follow his teachings all our lives, we pray in Christ's name. Amen.

The Moments of Silent Meditation

The Lord's Prayer *(in unison)*

The Gift of Music and Talents

Scripture   Matthew 2:1-2, 7-12

Presentation of the Gift of Music and Talents

We hear the music of Christmas as it chimes from church steeples to the bells of the Salvation Army kettles. We hear it on the radio, in concert halls, and shopping malls. For the past thirty days we have heard the same tunes until they violated our senses. And yet, when we gather together and sing the beautiful carols of Christmas, a flood of emotions overwhelms us and the carols sound as new and fresh as ever!

With pride we watch the school children as they develop in poise, talents, and ability. We delight in the creative ability of writers, musicians, actors, and artists. We are even amazed when the creative juices flow through our own veins as we give of our talents.

So I present the Gift of Music and Talents in appreciation for what we have been given, and as an offering to the Christ Child.

Special Music   "O Holy Night" (Adams)

The Gift of Joy

Scripture   Luke 1:68-72, 78-79

Presentation of the Gift of Joy

The gift of joy often comes to us in many small ways: it's the "hello" you never expected; it's the card from long-lost friends; it's the neighbor sharing homemade bread. It is also the squeal of laughter, the clapping of hands, and the stillness, the quiet moments before a fireplace, the decorating of the Christmas tree, and watching someone open the special gift you made.

Joy also comes to us when we see the scarlet color of the cardinal as it sits on a snow-covered branch. It is the feeling of contentment when we have done a job well. It is happiness in being warm and comfortable and cared for.

I bring the Gift of Joy to the Tiny King because I know how much sorrow he will endure as the Messiah. Perhaps his childhood can be full of joy?

The Carol   "Joy To The World" (verses 1, 2, and 4)

The Gift of Love

Scripture   John 3:16-17; 2 Corinthians 8:9

Presentation of the Gift of Love

Love is a mother rocking her infant. Love is a parent caring and providing for the family. Love is the bond between man and woman. Love is the feeling between brother and sister. Love is friend walking with friend. Love is helping someone in need. Love is putting someone else's needs ahead of our own.

Love was when God became a man-child and came down to us at Christmas. Love was the sacrifice of God's Son that we all might live. Love was victory over sin and death.

To the Christ of Christmas I present the Gift of Love; my love to him, my pledge to serve him because of his love for me.

66

The Christmas Eve Meditation (Pastor)

The Candlelighting Ceremony
(while singing "Silent Night, Holy Night")

The Benediction

The Postlude

The Angels'
Point Of View

A Christmas Story
In Two Acts

Stephen A. Berger

Introduction

The Play

The first scene sets the stage for the play. It introduces the locale and the characters, and begins to explore the reasons for God's gift to the world. It introduces the first four angels, the first two of which are given the personalities of younger or less experienced angels. It is their job to ask the questions that provide the audience with a better understanding of the play. The Gospels of Saint Matthew and Saint Luke are the foundation for the play. Nearly all of the scriptural material used in the play comes from these books. In Act 1 Scene 2, the angelic visits to the parents of John and Jesus are described, and Gabriel's personality is set as not so tolerant. Act 1 Scene 3 takes the play through the birth of Jesus. However, the play does not climax here as most Christmas pageants do. This scene has all the cast on stage at once and foreshadows the second act.

Act 2 Scene 1 covers the Magi traveling to worship the Messiah, stopping at Herod's castle on the way. The second scene in the act takes place after the Magi have arrived and presented their gifts. The angels' visits to Joseph and the Magi, warning of Herod's threat, are presented here. And the Holy Family's escape to Egypt forms the climax of the play. The final scene relates Herod's death and hints of the horror he perpetrated on young Jewish boys. The Holy Family is brought back to Israel and the first two angels recap the events of the play for the audience. One of the angels indicates the feeling of many in the world, that now that's over and done with. But the other angel reminds us all that it was not an end, but the most incredible beginning ever.

Requirements

The cast is a minimum of thirteen angels. There are thirteen speaking roles of various sizes. However, there are always opportunities for adding more to the heavenly host. Except for the lines of the first two angels and Gabriel, most of the rest could be spread among larger numbers of angels if the play is being performed by a large cast. Further, extra nonspeaking angels in Act 1 Scene 3 are always welcome, and could easily also be inserted into other scenes as two or more angels walking by a conversation being held by the speaking roles. However, performing the play with less than thirteen would be tricky. All thirteen speaking roles are on stage in Act 1 Scene 3 at one time and all have at least one line in that scene. It could be arranged that the role of either angel 7 or 8 could be performed by angel 3 or 4, but it would take some creative effort to make it seamless.

There are speaking roles with more or less lines than others. Angels 1 and 2 have fairly large roles, as does Gabriel. Angels 7 and 8 have the least lines. In this manner, those who like more lines and who can handle larger parts can be matched with what suits them best. And the shy student can usually be convinced to take one of the less demanding roles. Some shy students may prefer nonspeaking roles or not wish to participate in giving the play. This is not a problem. These students can construct scenery, props, and costumes. They can run lights or music and videotape the performance for the cast to see, or work on any event you may schedule with the play, such as a covered dish supper. Further, the play is designed to be a teaching tool for the class, such that hearing fellow students read their parts provides several lessons' worth of material.

Scenery

Go to a local appliance dealer and get as many refrigerator, stove, or other large appliance boxes as they can give you. This supply will prove useful in building your set and the only major prop, the star. On one box mark out a very large, six-pointed star with a pencil. This star should be large enough so that two angels can carry it, about three to four feet in diameter. Cut this out and paint it gold. Of the other boxes cut out large "clouds." You should make a class event of this. Collapse the boxes and cut one seam to open them flat with the writing down. The angels can all take shades of blue paint and swirl them together on the boxes. Glitter can be dropped on it, while the paint is wet, to create a nice effect.

After the paint dries (the following class) the clouds can be cut from the cardboard. Clouds that sit on the floor should have one flat side. Hanging clouds should be "scalloped" on all four sides. You will want one to be long and just tall enough to cover the chairs, used to support it and for angels to sit on. Another should be tall enough that an angel can stand on a chair behind it and be seen by the audience from about the waist up. Another(s) can be hung above the stage. The remaining clouds can be arranged at will, depending on how many you have and what sort of space you have as a stage. A light blue background (a couple of flat sheets) behind the clouds completes the entire set.

The two clouds with chairs behind them for sitting in or standing on are supported directly by one or more of the chairs. The cardboard clouds can be attached directly to the chairs with duct/masking tape. I recommend attaching one very stable chair sideways behind a tall cloud for Gabriel's podium in Act 1 Scene 3, and two short chairs, facing each other, to either end of a long, low cloud. Then two additional chairs for angelic seating can be placed behind the cloud facing the audience, pulled out for seated scenes and tucked in-between the two supporting chairs for standing scenes.

If you have no actual stage (as we did not), try setting up a couple of room dividers, or something equivalent on either side of your acting area, to create a stage-like framing of the space and to provide for entrances and exits.

Costumes

Costumes can be made of white and off-white flat sheets. Make an appeal to the congregation a month or more before the play, and have someone prepared to sew some quick seams for sides and sleeves and cut a hole out for the head. Fold the sheet in half and sew two "L" shapes on the corners (away from the fold) and cut out the corners. Done right, this should create a "T"-shaped piece of doubled cloth, with the fold at top of the "T." Cut a small semicircle at the center of the fold, making the head hole for your oversized "T"-shirt. Invert to hide the seams and the robe is done.

Haloes can be made of many things. We found that a stiff, wide gold ribbon, tied around the head worked well. The angels liked the headband look. Another idea we tried was to use two gold pipe cleaners to make a gold band to sit on the head. These look a bit more angelic, but they can fall off and aren't visible very far away.

We didn't make wings, but one angel brought some glitter makeup from home and wound up applying it on anyone who'd let her. It looked great.

Props

The star is the only required prop of the play. It should be small enough to move easily, but large enough so at least two angels look appropriate carrying it. Three or four feet wide works well. In Act 2 Scene 1, the angels carry it while delivering their lines. Between that scene and the next it is fixed in the set. We accomplished this by hanging it, with paper clip hooks, over the edge of a divider used to create side stage. Paper clip hooks are made by twisting large paper clips into "S" shapes and then pushing one end into the cardboard and using the other to hang the object up. We used these hooks to hang our suspended clouds on a rope strung across above the stage as well.

Although no other props are needed to perform the play, we found that Bibles carried by the angels make great disguises for copies of the play. Angel 2 also found that she liked slamming it closed at the end of her last line at the end of the play. Killing the lights at the same moment added to the effect. But much of this is serendipitous — let the class find its own humor and way of doing things. Everything here is a guide, and can be followed closely to create a very nice performance but there are equally rewarding paths to be found by starting to read parts out loud and asking the class what they think about props, sets, and costumes.

Overall

We performed this piece with taped music of the "Hallelujah Chorus," and also used soft music between scenes, while angels changed positions and the star got hung, and so on. Also we dimmed the lights at the end of each scene to indicate time passing. Since we combined the play with a covered dish supper, we had a ten-minute break at the intermission for refreshing. However, this can be shortened if circumstances suggest. Other events can be combined as well. We had live music performed during the intermission, collected donated toys for children, and had a carol sing afterwards.

The Angels' Point Of View

A Christmas Story In Two Acts

Act 1

Scene 1

(Clouds. Angels 1 and 2 sitting and talking. Since the entire play takes place in the clouds, it is possible to rearrange the clouds between scenes to create the impression that the time and location have changed. Other needed props and costumes include a large star that takes two to four angels to carry, robes, and halos. Harps and wings are optional)

1: Were you at last week's all-angel meeting?

2: No, I was busy with new arrivals at the gate. We can't shut down heaven for meetings, you know.

1: You should've been there. He was all upset. He kept saying *(in a deep voice)*, "I try to be just and merciful, but they simply don't listen."

2: Oh, brother, I know what you mean. I've heard Him say that many times. Been there, done that.

1: Yeah, but this time He was even getting down on the Scribes and Pharisees, you know, the religious leaders — His people.

2: Was He discouraged?

1: No, but He seemed pretty angry.

2: Man, I hope He doesn't do the Noah thing again. What a mess!

1: I don't think so. He was sad for ages and swore He'd never destroy the earth again, no matter how bad the people acted.

2: What do you think He'll do then?

1: I honestly have no idea. There's a rumor that it may be time for the Messiah that's been promised by the prophets.

2: That would be great. Maybe He'll send Michael. Mike's good with a sword and tosses a mean lightning bolt as well.

1: Yeah, he'd put the fear of God into those sinful humans.

(Angels 3 and 4 enter. They find space in the clouds and sit down)

3: Have you heard?

2: Heard what?

4: How God's going to deal with the people's sins.

1: We were just discussing that. We think He ought to send Michael to knock a little sense into them.

3: Well, you're certainly not the only angels who think so. The people seem so ungrateful sometimes and don't give Him the praise He deserves. I just don't ...

4: *(Interrupts)* Yeah, but that's not what God's going to do!

2: Then tell us — tell us!

1: Come on, don't hold out! Spill it!

3: He's going to send ...

3 and 4: His Son!

2: *(Long pause)* No, really. What is He going to do?

4: He's going to send His Son to teach the people.

1: Look, I wasn't just created yesterday. He doesn't have a Son!

3: Don't you remember the prophets Ezekiel, Isaiah, and the rest? You know, the Messiah prophecy.

2: Yeah, we know all that. We thought Michael would make a great messiah. I bet they'd all listen to him. And he could raise the people up, get rid of the Romans, and start a new strong line of kings.

1: A new leadership under someone like King David. King David wasn't perfect, but he wasn't too bad for a human.

4: No, no, no! You've got it all wrong. God isn't sending down a warrior. He's sending a lamb.

2: His Son is going to be a lamb?

4: *(Laughs)* No. I meant that His Son is to be like a lamb, sent to the sacrifice.

2: What?

1: You're telling us He is so upset with His creation that He is going to sacrifice His Son?

3 and 4: Yes.

(1 and 2 look at each other incredulously)

2: Let's leave this sacrificing bit for a moment. You still haven't told us where this Son is going to come from.

1: Yeah. This is the first time I've heard anything about any Son.

3: Well, this will take a little time, since God isn't going to just whip Him up and send Him down.

4: No. God has selected a young woman on Earth to bear His Son.

1: Lucky for us Earth time has very little meaning here.

2: Truly. Nine months of pregnancy, and then twelve long years until His bar mitzvah when He becomes a man, able to speak His Father's word in the temple.

3: Yes, it does take time, but God has His reasons. His Son must live as one of the people in order to truly understand them.

4: And His sacrifice would not mean as much, if He weren't one of them.

1: There you go about this "sacrifice" again.

2: Yeah. What's up with that?

4: You guys really ought to read up on your prophecies, you know that? The Messiah is supposed to come from the House of David, to be born in a place called Bethlehem, and is to be a sacrifice for the sins of the world.

(1 and 2 look impressed, but puzzled)

3: Couldn't have said it better myself!

2: Wait a second there! Did you just say the Messiah is to come from the House of David?

4: Yep.

1: And didn't you also say he was to be the Son of God?

3: Yes, and I think I see where you're going with this. God will be His father, but His mother's husband will be from the House of David.

4: As you know, the people trace their line through the male head of household. And so the prophecy is fulfilled.

2: But why does the Messiah have to be sacrificed?

1: I think I know why. Only through the ultimate sacrifice of death can God hope to illustrate that coveting worldly things above all else is to lose one's life with Him forever. *(Short pause)* But sacrificing everything in pursuit of God will save them.

Scene 2
(Gabriel and Angels 5 and 6 standing among the clouds)

Gabriel: I'm glad that's over.

5: Glad what's over?

Gabriel: My third visit to the Earth this year.

6: Wow! Something must be up if *you've* been to Earth three times that quickly.

Gabriel: It's the birth of God's Son at last.

5: What do you have to do with that?

6: *(Turns to 5)* Well, Gabriel is His messenger, after all.

5: *(Faces 6)* But He hasn't actually been born yet — so what's the message?

Gabriel: If you'll just be silent a second, I'll tell you.

(Gabriel pauses while 5 and 6 turn back to face him)

Gabriel: It all started about six months ago. An older woman, named Elizabeth, had no child, and she and her husband, the priest Zechariah, wanted one dearly. God had a purpose in mind for a certain man and selected these two to be his parents. So, of course it falls to old Gabriel to go down to tell Zechariah the good news. Piece of cake, I thought. He'll be incredibly grateful. Boy, was I wrong!

6: Why?

5: What happened?

Gabriel: Well ... Zechariah didn't believe me.

6: You're kidding!

Gabriel: No. I'm not.

5: What chutzpah! *(Pronounced "hoods-pa")*

6: What did you say?

5: What did you *do*?

Gabriel: What could I do? I struck him dumb for not believing God could and would make it come true.

6: Forever?

Gabriel: No! ... Just until his child is born. He only doubted a little. He is truly a good man and a good friend to God. Why else would he be selected to sire this child?

5: Just who is this child anyway?

6: Yeah, it can't be the Messiah. His mother's name is Mary, or so I've heard.

Gabriel: His name is John and he is to prepare the way for the Messiah. And you're right about the Messiah's mother's name. She was the subject of my second trip to Earth.

5: Oh, boy, I can just imagine that conversation. How did you tell her?

Gabriel: Well, first I had to overcome her fear.

6: Why? What happened?

Gabriel: I honestly don't know. I just appeared to her and said, "Greetings, favored one. God is with you. You are truly blessed among women," and told her she had been chosen to bear God's only Son. Then she started shaking.

5: Gee, you'd think she'd be elated, getting a message like that from you, Gabriel.

Gabriel: You're not going to believe this, but she started looking a bit skeptical and said, "But, I am a virgin. How is it that I am to give birth?" I don't mind telling you, I thought I was going to have another Zechariah on my hands.

6: So what did you do?

Gabriel: I simply told her what God had done for her cousin Elizabeth, and ...

5: Her cousin?

Gabriel: Oh, yeah, didn't I mention that? Elizabeth and Mary are cousins. Neat coincidence, eh?

6: I don't think He ever does anything by coincidence. Anyway, get back to the story.

Gabriel: I tell Mary that old barren Elizabeth, she-who-everybody-thought-would-never-have-a-child, is six months pregnant. Then I drive it home by saying, *(with emphasis)* "For nothing is impossible for God!" After that, she was a bit more believing and grateful, believe me.

6: You certainly had a rough time for someone with such great messages.

5: But you know what they say, no one ever likes the messenger.

Gabriel: Still, though — those two were a breeze. This last one was the toughest of all.

5: Why?

6: Who did you visit?

Gabriel: My last visit was to Mary's fiancé.

6: Oh, my!

Gabriel: "Oh, my" is right. His name is Joseph and when he found out that his bride-to-be was pregnant, he decided to un-engage himself quietly and go elsewhere. It's not easy to convince a man to marry a pregnant virgin.

5: I imagine not!

6: Oh, how could he disown God's firstborn Son? He should be grateful for the incredible honor paid to him!

5: Well, he can't be too bad of a man. At least he didn't publicly declare her an adulterer and try to have her stoned, like many might have done.

Gabriel: True enough.

5: So how did you convince him?

6: Yeah, what did you say?

Gabriel: The hard part was getting him past the shock. Once I got him calmed down a bit, he was a lot more reasonable. And after I explained it all to him, how God had planned it and the prophets had ordained it and all, he was actually happy to oblige.

5: *(Turns to 6)* See, told you he wasn't too bad.

6: And that was that?

Gabriel: Oh, yeah. There was one other thing. I told him that the child's name would be Jesus or Savior, and that He would be called Emmanuel.

6: That's beautiful. What's it mean?

Gabriel: It means "God with us."

Scene 3

(Clouds. Three small groups of angels, four or five in each, talking quietly to each other as background noise. They will be saying things like "I'm so excited." "It's finally time." "I just knew He was going to be cute." "Everyone's been practicing their harps all week." One at a time the individual groups' conversations come to the forefront and are heard over all)

[First Group]
5: Wow. It seems like just yesterday, when Gabriel was telling us about his visits to the Earth.

6: Yeah and now it's nearly time for the baby's birth!

7: You mean *Jesus'* birth?

8: Yes, God wants us all to call Him by His names.

6: There are certainly enough to choose from.

5: Gabriel mentioned two, Jesus and ...

6: Emmanuel! I remember how I thought that name was so beautiful.

7: The "Son of God" ...

8: ... and the "Son of Man."

5: And don't forget the "Lamb."

7: Or the "Messiah."

8: Yes. They are all good names for the one who has come to save the Earth.

[Second Group]

1: I heard that they're getting a group of angels together to go to the east when the baby Jesus is born.

2: I wonder why.

1: They say there are three wise sages or magi from the east who will come to pay homage to the baby Jesus. Angels are needed to guide them through unfamiliar territory, across wide deserts.

3: I can't imagine going away just when things are getting started here.

4: Me either. I want to be here watching every moment. This doesn't happen every millennium, you know.

1: If God asked you, you would go.

4: Of course, if He wanted us to go, we'd know it was important and there would be no questions asked. Still, I'd be sad to leave just now.

2: So would I.

3: Me, too.

[Third Group]

9: So why were we all called here?

10: It's the birth of God's Son!

9: I *know* that, but that won't be for a little while yet, and besides why would she be having the baby out here in the middle of a pasture? I just want to know why we're *here*.

11: She won't be.

9: *(Turns to face 11)* She won't be what?

11: Having the baby out here.

12: That's right. I heard she's going to give birth to God's Son in a stable!

9: This is a joke, right?

11: It's no joke. He will be born in a stable and wrapped in swaddling cloths to sleep in a manger.

10: With the ox and the sheep to sing Him a lullaby.

9: Okay. I understand all that. But that still doesn't explain why we're right here — right now.

12: Actually it does. Being born in a stable doesn't make you easy to find, which is good in some ways, but bad in others.

10: What do you mean?

12: If you're coming to worship God's Son, it's not a good thing if you can't find Him. But if you're seeking Him to do Him harm, being hard to find can be very useful.

10: Who would have the nerve to try to harm God's Son?

12: There are many who would like to see the Messiah killed before his time.

11: Yes. Do not forget the powers available to our brother Lucifer and the fallen angels he has taken away from us.

10: Would he go that far in defying God?

12: I would not put it past him.

9: All right. So what does this all have to do with us being here now?

11: Easy. We are here to lead the worshipers to the stable.

(Gabriel enters and gets ready to organize the angels for singing to the shepherds)

Gabriel: It's show time! Is everybody ready?

2: Everybody is way past ready!

3: *(Turns to address all of the angels, calling out)* Okay, everyone. Gabriel has something to say. So listen up.

Gabriel: It's time! If you don't know the words by now, it's too late. Sopranos in the front — basses in the back — and everybody else in between. *(Angels start getting into a single, large group)* Let's go now. Come on, there's enough room for everyone.

1: *(To 2)* Who are we doing this for anyway? Some kings and priests?

2: No. I think they said we're singing to some "shepherds."

4: That's right. Since God's Son is to be a Lamb, who is more fitting to welcome His first cries than the shepherds?

1: When you put it like that, I can't argue with you.

3: Come on, you guys! Let's join the others.

(All Angels exit singing Hallelujah or use lip sync to Handel's "Hallelujah Chorus" — either way, fade to end Act 1)

Intermission

Act 2

Scene 1

(Clouds. Four angels carrying a very large star)

10: Gee, I wonder how Jesus is doing.

12: He's doing just fine. Keep your mind on our task.

9: No big deal. We just use this star as a signal beacon and the three Wise Men follow us. No problem.

11: What about the *other* part of the job?

9: Huh?

10: *(To 9)* He means the protecting.

12: Yes. That's a very important part of our task.

9: I still find it hard to believe anyone would actually seek to harm the Son of God.

11: You'd better not let Gabriel hear you talk like that. He's not real patient with doubters.

10: Hey, look! The Magi are stopping at that castle over there.

9: They must be tired and seeking comfortable rooms for the night.

12: This could be trouble. That's King Herod's castle.

9: So. Why's that a problem?

11: Many think that the Messiah will be a king sent to rule over Israel. Herod is a jealous king, even if his rival is ordained by God Himself.

10: You're right. The Wise Men are asking Herod about a baby being born, who is to be the King of the Jews.

12: Did you see his reaction? There is no doubt whose side Herod is on.

11: Yes, the snake! Did you hear? Herod told them to go and search his realm and then come back to tell him where the baby is.

12: He even told them that he wants to be able to worship the new King himself. And they fell for it.

9: We'd better tell Gabriel about this when we get back.

10: How far is it to Bethlehem?

12: Not far now.

11: We should be there in just a couple more days.

10: I wonder how the baby Jesus is doing? It seems like forever since He was born.

12: Don't worry. He'll be only *twelve* days old when you see Him next — not an old man by anybody's measure.

9: Let's get going. The Wise Men are ready to travel again.

Scene 2
(Clouds. The star is now fastened in place. Angels 9, 10, and 11 are sitting and talking)

10: Wow! Those eastern sages bring nice gifts!

9: They certainly do honor the Son of God.

10: Gold, frankincense, and myrrh. Very appropriate gifts for a Prince.

11: Yes, but perhaps not so useful to a baby.

(Angel 12 enters)

12: Oh, they'll prove very helpful, don't you worry.

9: Did you tell Gabriel about Herod?

12: *(Sits down)* Yes. Gabriel said that it wasn't a problem. Herod was bound to find out sooner or later, and if not Herod, Lucifer would have found another tool.

10: And here I thought we had done something to help protect the child.

12: We have! Don't you see it?

11: Of course! Why didn't I see it before?

10: *(To 11)* What are you talking about?

9: I get it!

10: Well, will somebody please tell me?

12: Our assignment was to bring the worshipers from the east, whose gifts can help a young family in exile.

9: Will they have to flee?

(Gabriel enters)

Gabriel: Yes. Herod is already plotting to kill the child.

10: How can King Herod, the leader of God's people, be this way?

Gabriel: Herod is bitter and jealous. He wants no king over him.

11: What if the Wise Men tell King Herod where Jesus is? What if Herod gets here before the family can flee?

Gabriel: I will go to the eastern sages and warn them not to return to Herod before going home and I'll also warn Joseph and Mary that they must move on as soon as mother and child can travel safely.

Scene 3
(Four angels — 5, 6, 7, and 8 — stand and talk together)

5: I thought he'd never go.

6: He really wasn't that old.

8: Well, he certainly ruled long enough for me.

(Other angels nod and murmur their agreement. Four more angels — 1, 2, 3, and 4 — enter and join the group)

7: Hi. I guess you all heard the news?

1: About King Herod dying? Yeah, we heard.

3: He certainly was an evil man.

6: I know. I couldn't believe it when I heard him condemn all those innocent children to death, just to be sure that Jesus was one of them.

4: Hearing it wasn't nearly as horrible as seeing it.

2: I couldn't watch. It made me sick.

1: I hope the world never witnesses such a horrible evil again.

5: Who doesn't?

8: Is it really over?

7: Herod's dead and there really aren't many more young boys left in Israel anyway.

3: Herod's son, Archelaus, is no prize. He's nearly as bad as his father.

(Gabriel and all remaining Angels enter)

Gabriel: Well, we've brought them back to Israel.

6: The child is back? Jesus is back?

Gabriel: Do you doubt me?

6: *(A little hurriedly)* No, no. I'm just overwhelmed with joy! Emmanuel has returned!

4: I hope Archelaus doesn't find Him. He may treat Jesus as badly as his father wanted to.

Gabriel: I warned Joseph about that little problem and we led them all to safety in Galilee, far from Herod's son. They're living in a little place called Nazareth. After all, the prophets said that the Messiah would be called a Nazarene.

(Angels all nod in agreement and start to disperse in little groups of two to four, talking and nodding as they exit. Eventually only angels 1 and 2 are left)

1: It's finally over.

2: What do you mean?

1: The family and Messiah are safe. They are back in Israel again, Herod's dead, the shepherds and Wise Men are long back in their homes ... It's done. We did a good job, but it's over.

2: You must be kidding. This isn't even the beginning.

1: What do you mean?

2: Well, the Lamb must still grow up and teach God's people. And He must be sacrificed to redeem from sin all those who believe in Him and love God.

1: It makes me so sad.

2: Don't be sad. And wait. Mark my words. Jesus will surely stir up a tornado with His teaching *(slight pause)*, but it will only be after He defeats death that things really heat up. And that doesn't even include the second coming.

1: What second coming?

2: Now, that's another story.

The End

In Search
Of Christmas

A Christmas Drama

Eulonda A. Dreher

Introduction

With a series of brief dialogues between a husband and wife, two teenagers, two weary women, and others, the congregation catches poignant glimpses of how we can get off track and lose the real meaning of Christmas.

Interspersed with these negative dialogues are uplifting, faith affirming conversations between individuals who have maintained the spirit of joy and giving during the Christmas season.

Scriptural and musical interludes are included throughout. Music may be added or omitted at the director's discretion.

This is a light, contemporary drama for the Christmas season. It can be performed in a church setting, school, or other place where there is a platform, stage, or auditorium. Cast includes Guide, Searcher, Reader, and several individuals to produce the six dialogues; each dialogue contains two or three scenes (individuals may do more than one dialogue).

Setting

Christmas tree in center of stage with room scene on each side to make two dialogue areas.

Props Needed

Table with chairs, lamp, recliner or overstuffed chair, coffee cups, telephone and stand, coat rack with coat and gloves, a tool box, and other items to make two scenes which appear to be rooms in a home. The tree should be decorated and have wrapped boxes underneath.

The set and props are easily managed, and a small number of actors is required for the cast, if some actors take more than one part. It is somewhat abstract with the intangible "search" for Christmas and is ultimately a search of the heart and spirit for the true meaning of Christmas as well as attitudes that make Christmas a blessing rather than an endurance of a series of traditional activities.

In Search Of Christmas

Setting
Platform divided into two focus centers, left and right, each set as a room in a home, i.e., table with coffee cups, chairs, lamps, recliner, and so on. Decorated Christmas tree in the center of set.

(Center stage, on lower level, Searcher is looking at a map. Spotlight on Searcher. Guide enters)

Guide: Hey, goin' somewhere? What are you looking for?

Searcher: I'm trying to find Christmas.

Guide: Well, you won't find it on a map. Here, let me give you some directions. You see, Christmas is in different places for different people. Know what I mean? *(Searcher shakes head no, with a puzzled look)* It just depends on your perspective. Anyway, just as you pass Thanksgiving, you're into Christmas. Now, this is where it gets confusing. You see, Christmas is located where your heart is.

Searcher: Wait a minute; where my heart is? You're right, I'm confused. You mean I have to find my heart, before I can find Christmas?

(Spotlight fades)

Music

(Spotlight on Guide and Searcher)

Guide: It's easy to find Christmas if you just follow the road signs. But if you want to find the real Christmas, you have to follow the path directed by God.

Searcher: Whoa, you're getting way ahead of me. I need better directions than that.

Guide: Okay. Let's eavesdrop a little. Maybe this will help.

Dialogue 1
(Spotlight left, two ladies enter and begin dialogue as they approach center of set)

Scene 1
Speaker 1: Well, here it is December again. Every year I promise myself that I'll get better organized with my shopping, baking, decorating — you know, all those things you have to do for Christmas.

Speaker 2: There's plenty of opportunity to get an early start. There are signs of Christmas in the stores before we get our summer clothes put away.

Speaker 1: And every year, there is more and more entertaining to do. Between concerts, dinner parties, open houses, and programs, the rest of our life gets put on hold.

Speaker 2: Not to mention having to make those ridiculous costumes. Cary is an "unwanted" Christmas tree in his third grade program. Have you ever made a Christmas tree costume out of a large trash bag and construction paper?

Speaker 1: Oh, well, Christmas will soon be over, and we can get on with our lives.

(Spotlight fades and moves to right stage)

Scene 2

Speaker 3: With all the activities, parties, programs, shopping — it's easy to forget why we really celebrate Christmas.

Speaker 4: There must be something we can do to keep our calendar in perspective and do it with a purpose — celebrating the greatest gift humans have ever received.

Speaker 3: I have an idea. This year we can use an Advent chain to recall the events leading to the birth of Jesus. Each day we will reflect on a portion of the real Christmas story to help us keep our other activities in perspective.

(Spotlight fades)

Reader: And the Word of the Lord says:
    "The days are coming, declares the Lord, when I will fulfill the gracious promise I made to the house of Israel and to the house of Judah. In those days and at that time, I will make a righteous Branch sprout from David's line: he will do what is just and right in the land." (Jeremiah 33:14-16)

(Spotlight back to Searcher and Guide)

Searcher: I think I'm catching on — maybe. On one hand, it sounds like Christmas is a calendar of events that one must attend on the way to Christmas. *(Still a little confused)* Yet, some of the events and activities are necessary to finding the "heart" of Christmas.

Guide: You're on the right track. Keep looking.

(Spotlight fades)

Music

Reader: And the Word of the Lord says:

"There are also heavenly bodies and there are earthly bodies; but the splendor of the heavenly bodies is one kind, and the splendor of the earthly bodies is another ... star differs from star in splendor." (1 Corinthians 15:40)

"... A star will come out of Jacob; a scepter will rise out of Israel." (Numbers 24:17b)

"Those who are wise will shine like the brightest of the heavens, and those who lead many to righteousness, like the stars for ever and ever." (Daniel 12:3)

Music

Reader: And the Word of the Lord says:

"Where is the one who has been born king of the Jews? We saw his star in the east and have come to worship him." (Matthew 2:2)

"... and the star they had seen in the east went ahead of them until it stopped over the place where the child was. When they saw the star, they were overjoyed." (Matthew 9b-10)

(Spotlight back to Guide and Searcher)

Guide: Why are you looking for Christmas anyway? Are you looking for friends, entertainment *(Sarcastically)*, or answers to the purpose of life? What?

Searcher: All of the above. Curiosity mainly. I've heard different opinions about Christmas and decided to find out for myself where Christmas really is and what the big "hype" is all about.

Guide: Well, you're right about different opinions. But, attitudes have a lot to do with it, too. Listen.

(Spotlight fades)

Dialogue 2
(Spotlight on left stage with two ladies sitting at the table having "coffee")

Scene 1
Speaker 1: Christmas is so depressing. It all seems so useless and unnecessary. All we do is go to a bunch of parties, buy gifts we can't really afford, receive gifts we don't really need, or want, and stuff ourselves with food that isn't good for us! Why? Sometimes I wish we didn't even have Christmas.

Speaker 2: I guess we just tolerate the traditions. What I dread is all that decorating. I spend a week getting Christmas decorations out and deciding what isn't worth using again, and where to put those things that are, then buying more. All for a few weeks, then putting it all away again.

(Spotlight fades)

Scene 2
(Spotlight on right stage with two ladies seated at the table having "coffee")

Speaker 3: Isn't Christmas so exciting? I love the joy and cheerfulness that seems to be more prevalent during Christmastime. The sparkle and shine of the lights remind me of the bright stars and glory of the heavens on that first Christmas night. Knowing that God fulfilled his promise to send the Messiah, helps me know he will keep all his promises. Doesn't that give you a special lift?

Speaker 4: I'll say it does. That's why I love the star on the top of my Christmas tree. It reminds me of God's promise — the Savior.

(Spotlight fades, then goes back to Searcher and Guide)

Searcher: I see what you mean about attitudes and perspectives. I'm wondering if Christmas is in two different places.

Guide: You're catching on. It goes back to what I said about "where your heart is." If your heart is in the world, Christmas can be quite a burden from which you want to escape. If your heart is in tune with God, Christmas brings promise, hope, peace — all that good stuff.

Searcher: I get it. Christmas is just at the end of the year for some; for others it's a reminder of where life begins — and never ends.

Guide: You're on your way.

(Spotlight fades)

Music

Reader: And the Word of the Lord says:
" 'The days are coming,' declares the Lord, 'when I will raise up to David a righteous Branch, a King who will reign wisely and do what is just and right in the land.' " (Jeremiah 23:5)
"A shoot will come up from the stump of Jesse; from his roots a Branch will bear fruit. The Spirit of the Lord will rest on him — the Spirit of wisdom and of understanding, the Spirit of counsel and of power, the Spirit of knowledge and of the fear of the Lord ... Righteousness will be his belt, and faithfulness the sash around his waist ... In that day the Root of Jesse will stand as a banner for the peoples; the nations will rally to him, and his place of rest will be glorious." (Isaiah 11:1-2, 5, 10)
"The virgin will be with child and will give birth to a son, and they will call him Immanuel — which means 'God with us.' " (Matthew 1:23)
"So Joseph also went up from the town of Nazareth in Galilee to Judea, to Bethlehem, the town of David ... While they were there, the time came for the baby to be born, and she gave birth to her firstborn, a son." (Luke 2:4a, 6b-7a)

(Spotlight back to Searcher and Guide)

Searcher: I think I'm getting closer to Christmas.

Guide: Good. Just be aware of the side roads that may lure you off track. For example ...

(Spotlight fades)

Dialogue 3
(Two teenage girls enter; spotlight on youth, left stage)

Scene 1

Speaker 1: *(Depressed)* I guess Christmas will be a real bust this year.

Speaker 2: Why? I thought you were excited about getting that new leather jacket.

Speaker 1: That's just it. My parents said it's too expensive. They'll probably get me some sweaters and a "cute" flannel nightgown. If I can't have what I really want, I'd rather they just didn't bother. After all, Christmas comes only once a year.

(Spotlight moves to right stage as two more teens enter)

Scene 2

Speaker 3: *(Cheerfully)* So, what are you getting for Christmas?

Speaker 4: Oh, I don't know. I like to be surprised. I've made a few suggestions, but I usually like whatever I get.

Speaker 3: It's really neat to see those little kids in the children's home receive the toys our group donates each year. Their faces just light up; you'd think they'd been given a million dollars.

Speaker 4: And taking cookies and fruit to those people in the nursing home brightens my spirit as well. We may be the only company some of them have during the holidays.

Speaker 3: Yeah, you're right. Giving is what Christmas is all about.

(Spotlight fades)

Reader: And the Word of the Lord says:
    "On coming to the house, they saw the child with his mother Mary, and they bowed down and worshiped him. Then they opened their treasures and presented him with gifts of gold and of incense and of myrrh." (Matthew 2:11)
    "... remembering the words of the Lord Jesus himself: 'It is more blessed to give than to receive.' " (Acts 20:35)

(Spotlight back to Searcher and Guide)

Searcher: Hmmm. Gift-giving and getting could lead one off track, couldn't it? Like they say — "It's not the gift but the thought that counts."

Guide: Right. Just keep in mind: we give because God gave his Son. Nothing compares to that as long as you give with a loving heart and a generous spirit. You're getting close to the real Christmas.

(Spotlight fades)

Music

Reader: And the Word of the Lord says:
   "Today in the town of David a Savior has been born to you; he is Christ the Lord. This will be a sign to you: you will find a baby wrapped in cloths and lying in a manger." (Luke 2:11-12)

(Spotlight on Guide and Searcher)

Guide: Christmas is named for the baby Jesus — the Christ who became the Savior of the world.

Searcher: That's interesting. Then why is Santa so popular at Christmas?

Guide: Well, he adds to the scenery at Christmas. He also provides an opportunity for creativity and imagination. There's nothing wrong with a little fun along the way.

(Spotlight fades)

Dialogue 4
(Spotlight on left stage with two mothers discussing plans)

Scene 1
Speaker 1: I'm so exhausted, but I have to take the kids to see Santa this afternoon. After all, Christmas is for kids. I can't deprive them of seeing Santa. That's what it's all about.

Speaker 2: Be prepared, the line will be forever. There goes your afternoon. You won't get any shopping done today.

Speaker 1: Well, I'll have the rest of the week. I'm still not sure what to get for Jeremy. And I still need a few stocking stuffers.

(Spotlight fades and moves to right stage where one person, holding a handmade ornament, stands)

Scene 2
Speaker: Giving gifts at Christmas is so special. Sometimes the smallest gifts are the most precious. I remember some handcrafted gifts that have become real treasures. Santa even brought a few of them. They become the material markers that remind us of what is really important — reminders of the greatest love ever given.

(Spotlight fades as speaker places ornament on the tree. Spotlight then goes to a child on left stage)

Scene 3

Speaker 1: *(Seated at a desk writing a letter)* Dear Santa: I'm looking forward to your visit. I think I've been very good this year. My grades have been mostly *A*'s and *B*'s and I've only been grounded twice. I've made a list of several things I'd like to have. If you can't bring it all, I'll understand. I've put the things I want most at the top of the list. My little sister has a list, too, but she can't write yet. Please bring her some things, too. It would be nice if you'd also bring something for Mom and Dad. Mom and I will make cookies before you visit, so I'll leave some on the table for you along with a glass of milk. By the way, Santa, do you know the Wise Men who took gifts to baby Jesus when he was born? Every year, I wonder if that's why you bring gifts to us — to help us remember the gifts of the Wise Men. It was nice of them to honor Jesus on his birthday. I try to honor Jesus, too, by doing nice things for others.

I hope you have a safe trip. I'll be expecting you on Christmas Eve.

Speaker 2: *(Seated at desk writing a letter)* Dear Santa: I hope you can remember who I am. There were so many kids talking to you last week. I'm the one who wants a red bike and a PlayStation with games. Mom said we shouldn't be too particular though about the gifts. We should be happy with whatever you bring. And Dad said giving gifts is just as important as receiving them. Well, I bought a remote control car with my own money for my friend, Danny. But I'd still like to have the bike and PlayStation. We don't have a chimney or fireplace, so you'll have to use the back door. Our Christmas tree is in the living room and has a lot of lights and ornaments on it.

(Spotlight fades, then goes back to Searcher and Guide)

Searcher: That does sound like fun. And not just for kids. I think grown-ups like Santa, too.

Guide: I'm sure they do. If you keep him in the right perspective, you'll still get to the real Christmas.

(Spotlight fades)

Music

Reader: And the Word of the Lord says:
"May the God of hope fill you with all joy and peace as you trust in him, so that you may overflow with hope by the power of the Holy Spirit." (Romans 15:13)
"But may the righteous be glad and rejoice before God; may they be happy and joyful." (Psalm 68:3)
"But may all who seek you rejoice and be glad in you; the Lord be exalted!" (Psalm 40:16)

(Spotlight on Searcher and Guide)

Searcher: I'm beginning to see the real Christmas. I think I can find my way now.

Guide: Good. Christmas is really wonderful. Once you find it, you'll find peace, joy, excitement, and cheer. But don't be misled. Watch out for traps.

Searcher: Traps?

(Spotlight fades)

Dialogue 5
(Spotlight on left stage where two men are seated)

Scene 1

Speaker 1: Well, since it's Christmas, I guess I should show a little good will. Maybe, I'll help Sam next door shovel the snow from his driveway. I just hope I don't throw my back out again. It's all I can do to get my own driveway cleared.

Speaker 2: That is a lot of work for someone with a bad back. And it isn't a quick job, either. Why don't you just send him a nice Christmas card? Maybe stick in a ticket to the basketball game.

Speaker 1: I don't know. Those tickets aren't easy to come by, and they are rather expensive. Maybe Joan will bake some cookies or Christmas bread for them. That would be a gesture of good will, don't you think? *(Speaker 2 nods in agreement)*

(Spotlight moves to right stage where two men are seated)

Scene 2

Speaker 3: Hey, Paul, Merry Christmas. I hear you're going to visit your kids for Christmas. I know you're anxious to see the grandkids, too.

Speaker 4: Oh, we can't wait. It has been six months since we've seen them. Sandy said Katie is almost walking now. We'll be gone about two weeks.

Speaker 3: If you'd like, Kay and I will be glad to look after your house while you're away — get the mail and newspapers, water plants, feed your pets — whatever. Don't be concerned about things here. We'll keep a good watch. Just enjoy your trip. We'll know how to get in touch with you if we need too.

(Spotlight fades, then goes to a couple carrying a bag of groceries and shopping bag of boxes entering from the back. They are chattering to themselves. Spotlight catches them as they near the front and continue to stage)

Scene 3

Wife: *(Relieved)* That's it; I think the Christmas shopping is finished.

Husband: It better be — if you want to eat next month! We may have to cancel our ski trip. The car needs new tires and the furnace is making a funny noise.

Wife: Oh, well, I can't worry about those things.

Husband: You sure are in a cheerful mood.

Wife: It's Christmas! I won't let myself get depressed over things I can't control. Honey, will you put away those groceries? I have to get over to the church to work on the baby blankets for the shelter.

Husband: Again? You've been over there two nights this week.

Wife: Yes, but it's worth it to see the joy such small gifts bring to those young mothers who have so little for their babies. You should get involved, too. They need some men to help seal the windows and do some minor repairs on the building.

Husband: I don't know. I don't have time for that.

Wife: Okay, you stay here and worry about paying our bills. *(Exits)*

Husband: *(Thoughtfully)* It's true. I do worry about things I can't change or control. That's depressing. Maybe I should start thinking about how I could help others. I know how to seal windows. *(Calls to wife)* Wait, honey. Let me get my tools. *(Picks up tool box and exits)*

(Spotlight fades, then goes back to Searcher and Guide)

Searcher: I'm beginning to see why Christmas is difficult to find. It is a matter of knowing where your heart is. I want to find the real Christmas.

Guide: You're catching on quickly. You'll get there if you stay on the right track.

(Spotlight fades)

Music

Reader: And the Word of the Lord says:
   "Suddenly a great company of the heavenly host appeared with the angel, praising God and saying, 'Glory to God in the highest, and on earth peace to men on whom his favor rests.' " (Luke 2:13-14)
   "Shout for joy to the Lord, all the earth. Worship the Lord with gladness; come before him with joyful songs." (Psalm 100:1)

(Spotlight on Searcher and Guide)

Searcher: I can already feel the peace and comfort of Christmas. This is a wonderful place to be. Who wouldn't search for the real Christmas, the very heart of it?

Guide: Well, it isn't cheap here. In fact, Christmas can be quite costly, in more ways than one. Listen, you'll see what I mean.

(Spotlight fades)

Dialogue 6
(Spotlight on left stage, speaker glances around the room)

Scene 1

Speaker 1: *(Confidently and relieved)* It's hard to believe tomorrow is Christmas. Where does time go? All is well here. The gifts are all bought, wrapped, tagged, and under the tree — a beautiful tree I might add. Dinner is planned, the turkey is ready for the oven, all is ready for the final touch. The table is set with the best china and silver. Just 24 hours and this Christmas will be history, and it will take me most of next year to pay for it. Then, I start all over again.

(Spotlight moves to right stage where speaker is seated in a recliner, reading a newspaper. There is a table with a telephone beside the chair. A coat rack with a coat hanging on it is on the other side of the chair)

Scene 2

Speaker 2: *(Reading a newspaper article out loud)* Thursday, December 23. Family home destroyed by fire. Fire broke out in the living room of a small home on the north side of the city late last night. In spite of quick action from the fire department, the home was engulfed in flames and virtually destroyed. Fortunately, no one was injured. Mr. and Mrs. Henry DeVries and their two young daughters managed to escape unharmed. However, everything they owned was lost, including all of the family Christmas gifts. According to officials, the fire is blamed on a faulty string of lights on the Christmas tree. Mrs. DeVries, clutching a small Bible in one hand and her four-year-old daughter Emily in the other, escaped through the back door of the house. Mr. DeVries pulled seven-year-old Amanda from her bed, and they climbed to safety from the bedroom window. According to neighbors, the family had saved for several months to buy Christmas gifts for one another and for a few close relatives. At this time, housing for the family is being provided by members of First Baptist Church. Anyone interested in helping the DeVries can call the church for information. *(Puts newspaper down and dials the telephone)* Yes, I'm calling about the DeVries family. What kind of help is most needed at this time?

Speaker: *(Offstage)* Currently the family is staying in an apartment owned by a family of our church. The apartment was vacant, but had the minimum of furniture. At least they have shelter from the weather. We've given them food and clothing that had been collected here at the church, but that won't be enough for long. They are a very faithful, Christian family and are dealing with the situation, knowing that God will provide for them.

Speaker 3: What about Christmas? Is anyone providing for them especially tomorrow?

Speaker: *(Offstage)* I am not aware that anything other than the food which included some fresh produce and meat has been taken to them. Donations are being received at the church and will be delivered to the family immediately.

Speaker 3: My family would like to help. I'd like to see that they have some Christmas gifts. Would it be possible to have them delivered by Christmas morning? *(Hangs up the phone, puts on a coat and gloves, and proceeds to gather wrapped gifts from under the tree as he exits stage)*

(Spotlight fades, then goes back to Searcher and Guide)

Searcher: Wow! I'm beginning to see where my heart *should be* at Christmas. To have your heart in the right place does sometimes require sacrifice though, doesn't it?

Guide: Yes, it does. But consider the reward.

(Spotlight fades)

Reader: And the Word of the Lord says:
   "Do not store up for yourselves treasures on earth, where moth and rust destroy, and where thieves break in and steal. But store up for yourselves treasures in heaven, where moth and rust do not destroy, and where thieves do not break in and steal. For where your treasure is, there your heart will be also." (Matthew 6:19-21)

Music

Reader: And the Word of the Lord says:
   "For to us a child is born, to us a son is given, and the government will be on his shoulders. And he will be called Wonderful Counselor, Mighty God, Everlasting Father, Prince of Peace. Of the increase of his government and peace there will be no end. He will reign on David's throne and over his kingdom, establishing and upholding it with justice and righteousness from that time on and forever...." (Isaiah 9:6-7)
   "Worship the Lord in the splendor of his holiness; tremble before him, all the earth. Say among the nations, 'The Lord reigns.' " (Psalm 96:9-10)

(Spotlight goes back to Searcher and Guide)

Searcher: *(Excitedly)* I've found it; I've found the real Christmas: rejoice in the love of God; reflect on the gift of God — the promised Savior; focus on giving rather than receiving; sincerely put others first; be willing to make a sacrifice; and keep the spirit of Christmas in your heart all year — so you can find the real Christmas again next year!

Guide: Great! I couldn't have said it better myself. Enjoy the holidays, and — Merry Christmas!

Searcher: Thanks; same to you. *(Pulls out the map again)* Now, could you tell me how to find McDonald's? I'm starved.

(Searcher and Guide leave the stage together, looking at the map)

Congregation   "Joy To The World"

(All Scripture was taken from the New International Version of the Bible.)

Last Year In Bethlehem: The Story Of Eli The Shepherd

A Christmas Eve Service In One-Person Drama And Congregational Hymns

Russell W. Dalton

*This drama is lovingly dedicated to my wife
Lisa M. Dalton,
who always encourages me to take time to write and perform drama
as part of my ministry, then supports me in the effort,
and keeps me focused on why the story must be told.*

Introduction

Last Year In Bethlehem: The Story Of Eli The Shepherd reminds us that the story of Christ's birth is more than a holiday tradition. It is a story that can change lives, and it is a story that must be shared. Eli is a gruff, but friendly shepherd who is worldly-wise but has a new passion for life. On the first anniversary of the first Christmas, Eli shares the story of the night that changed his life. Along the way the congregation is invited to respond to his story through the singing of relevant, well-known Christmas carols.

This story appeals to young and old alike. It calls for only one actor, yet allows the entire congregation to participate through the singing of the hymns. There are minimal costuming requirements, and no set design requirements.

This drama can be used in a number of different ways. The order of worship provided uses the drama and singing as the sermon or message portion of the service. Alternatively, the drama and singing could come before a sermon during a Christmas Sunday or Christmas Eve service. *Last Year In Bethlehem* could also, after a brief welcome, stand alone as a special half-hour service.

The Christmas Eve Candlelighting Service provides calls for the congregation to sing all of the Christmas carols. But it would also be quite effective if one or two of these carols were sung by an adult or youth choir or by soloists.

The Church is called to carry on the memory and proclaim the message of Jesus Christ. One of the prime opportunities that we have to do this in the Church is through our Christmas services. This is an excellent time to tell the story to the community in a way that they can understand it. The gospel has always come to us in story form, and in our media-saturated electronic culture we are, just as in Jesus' day, once again living in a culture with eyes and ears for dramatic narrative. Because of this, drama is a vibrant, affective, and effective way to proclaim the good news to our neighbors at Christmastime. May God bless you as you tell the story.

An Historical Note On Shepherds In Jesus' Day

Sheep were a key commodity in Jesus' day. Sheep provided milk, food, wool, and covering for tents and were central to the sacrificial system of ancient times. As a result they were in many ways an important form of currency. There were many shepherds watching over flocks, so it is not possible to make any sweeping generalizations about shepherds. By some accounts shepherding was an honorable occupation. Shepherds in ancient times were hardworking people who worked long days outdoors, often sleeping in tents or other very basic shelter. They had to be diligent, and in a sense even nurturing to the helpless and vulnerable animals entrusted to their care. If they lost sheep, they were usually personally responsible to compensate the owners for the sheep. For Jewish shepherds there was also probably some pride and comfort to be found in the many biblical images of shepherding. By other accounts, however, shepherds in the first century were looked down upon as dishonest, unclean people. Shepherds worked long hours and therefore could not follow all of the ceremonial laws that other religious people did. Shepherds were often accused of supplementing their herds by steering other shepherds' sheep into their own flocks, and they often took the opportunity to lead their sheep onto other people's land for grazing without permission.

Shepherds often joined with other shepherds at a watering spot in the evening so that they could take turns keeping the night watch. Sheep knew the voice of their shepherds, so the herds would be easily separated in the morning by following the voices of the shepherds as they went their separate ways.

In the Gospel of Luke the presence of shepherds serves several purposes. Along with the setting of Bethlehem, the presence of shepherds recalls King David, a shepherd himself as a boy, to create a regal backdrop for the story. The presence of shepherds also recalls the many biblical images of God and God's chosen king as a shepherd caring for people. Perhaps most significantly, however, having shepherds hear the angel's proclamations and see the birth of the Messiah sets the tone for Luke's message that the Realm of God includes those who are often excluded from religious circles.

An Historical Note On Inns And Mangers

Luke's description of the birthplace of Jesus is very brief. The word "inn" could refer to any sleeping area, and does not necessarily refer to a commercial lodging house. A "manger" is a feeding trough, and not necessarily a whole stable. Many homes would have had their "inn," or sleeping area, upstairs or on a raised area of flooring. Cattle would have been kept under the same roof, downstairs or in the sunken room of a one-story home. It is likely that many of Joseph's relatives were traveling to a relative's home because of the census. Since the sleeping area would have been crowded, the best place to put a newborn baby may have been in the area where the animals were kept, and a feeding trough would be a natural makeshift cradle.

Suggestions For Costuming, Makeup, And Staging

The character of Eli should wear a basic robe with a rope or cloth tie. A member of the church can make this robe in the design of a simple shift out of some authentic-looking, solid fabric (black, white, or earth tones) from a sewing supply store. Contemporary bathrobes are not recommended. A shepherd's headdress is not necessary, but one can be made out of the same material as the robe by simply taking a piece of the cloth, wrapping it around the head, and tying it up with a headband of appropriate cloth. Eli should wear leather sandals on his feet. Plastic shower togs should be avoided.

Shaggy hair and a shaggy beard can add character to the role, but are not essential. A fake beard is not recommended. If floodlights are going to be used, some makeup can be used to give the impression of ruddy cheeks.

Eli should carry a shepherd's staff. This can be a hooked staff or simply a long walking stick made out of the branch of a tree. A knot on the end of this branch (which could then be used as a club) could add some authenticity, but is not necessary.

A bare stage area, with no other props or scenery, is recommended. (Sometimes attempts at scenery can actually distract from the illusion created by the actor/storyteller.)

A Christmas Eve Candlelighting Service

Gathering   "He Is Born, The Divine Child"

Carol   "Angels From The Realm Of Glory"

Scripture Reading   Luke 2:1-20

Lighting Of The Christ Candle

Welcome

Message In Drama And Hymns   "Last Year in Bethlehem: The Story Of Eli The Shepherd"
"O Little Town Of Bethlehem"   "Away In A Manger"
"People, Look East"   "What Child Is This?"
"O Come, O Come, Emmanuel"   "O Come, All Ye Faithful"
"Angels We Have Heard On High"   "Go Tell It On The Mountain"
"Silent Night"

The Christmas Offering

The Lighting Of The Candles
As "There's a Song in the Air" is sung, the church lights will be dimmed, and the minister will light a candle from the Christ candle. The minister then lights the candles of the ushers, who will light the candle of the first worshiper in each pew, and the light will be passed from worshiper to worshiper. Remember that the lighted candle remains upright, and the unlighted candle is tipped to the lighted candle. Please extinguish candles before leaving your seats and place them in the receptacle by the door upon leaving.

Carol   "There's A Song In The Air"

Prayer
O God of love and light, may the light of Jesus Christ shine through us this holiday season, and may the lives of those who feel in the dark be brightened by your love. We pray in our Savior's name. Amen.

Carol   "Joy To The World"

The Blessing

Sending Out   "Good Christian Friends, Rejoice"

Last Year In Bethlehem:
The Story Of Eli The Shepherd

Eli is a gruff, but friendly shepherd who is worldly-wise but has a new passion for life. He is dressed in a simple robe and sandals, and holds a shepherd's staff. He crosses to center stage to deliver his lines, but then steps to the side during the singing of each hymn.

Eli enters, looking up and off to his left. After a moment, he notices the congregation.

Oh, hullo. Didn't see you there. I was just looking up remembering what happened one year ago this night while I was watching the sheep. Hey, maybe I could tell you the story — *(With an apologetic bow for not introducing himself sooner)* Oh, my name is Eli, and yes, I'm a shepherd. Now I know shepherds don't have the best of reputations. People think of us as dirty and dishonest and such, and I won't deny that I've steered another shepherd's sheep over to my flock a time or two. But I remind you, King David was a shepherd, and maybe he watched his sheep right on this hillside same as me!

This is a story of Bethlehem, my hometown. You probably know it as the city of David. This is where David was born and grew up about 1,000 years ago. Often, when I'd be up here on the hillside watching my sheep, I'd look down over the city, and think about its famous past, and about its troubled present. Hmmf. My hometown of Bethlehem ... *(Suddenly breaks into a sly, proud grin)* Who'd have thought that the best was yet to come!

Carol   "O Little Town Of Bethlehem" (vv. 1-4)

Now, late that night a year ago, the streets of Bethlehem were finally deserted. Crowds had come from all over to our town because Augustus called for a tax. So all the streets were crowded, all the shops were crowded, the inns were crowded ... Well, you know how it is. I hope that doesn't become a tradition for this time of year. Well, it made for hectic, tiring days for most of the decent working folk of Bethlehem, and when night came most were fast asleep.

But of course me, I'm awake. Me and the shepherds with me had to take turns staying up watching the flock and keeping the fire going. So it's my turn. Brrr, and it's a cold night. And boring. There's nothing much to do but look east out over the city and wait for my shift to be over. So that's what I'm doing. Just looking east and waiting ...

Carol   "People Look East" (vv. 1-3)

I went to wake up the young man who was to take the next shift, but Nahum, he's already fidgeting and awake.

I said "Couldn't sleep, Nahum? What's wrong?"

And he says, "Oh, it aggravates me, Eli. Some pagan in Rome says, 'Boo,' and all the Jewish folk from all over have to jump. They have to travel all over."

"Ah, don't let it bother you, Nahum," I say. "Besides, those pious folk will need sheep to sacrifice. Ha! More business for us."

But Nahum, he just gets madder. He says, "All these people, they travel from all over just to have the great privilege of registering so that Rome can control them and collect taxes from them. And have them live in fear. Well, when the Messiah comes, we won't have to put up with it! I just have to believe the Lord God of Israel will send the Messiah soon, to rescue us from our oppressors. When the Messiah comes, we won't have to put up with Roman rule. When Messiah comes he will be our King!"

Nahum had a lot of faith; I'll give him that. But what he needed was a dose of reality. So I say to him, I say, "Now, Nahum, you don't get your hopes up too high. It'll just lead to disappointment and maybe even to getting into trouble. Some folks have been talking about the Messiah coming for years. But I don't see it happening. I'll give you this: you're right, these are hard times, troubled times. Not like in King David's day. *(Sighs)* If ever we could use a Messiah, we could use one now."

Carol   "O Come, O Come, Emmanuel"

Nahum, he's still agitated. He says to me, "But I tell you, Eli, the Messiah will come, soon! I feel it!"

I say, "And I feel cold and tired," and start to lie down to sleep, when all of a sudden ... *(Cries out)* LIGHT! *(Eli is frightened and shaky, and takes a couple of shaky breaths)* Blinding light! A MESSENGER OF GOD is standing right in front of us, and God's Glory shone around us.

(Eli drops his staff and falls to the floor) I fell on my face, shaking and terrified.

Then God's Messenger says, "Fear not."

(Almost sarcastically) "Yeah, right."

(Eli gets to his feet) But he goes on, "Fear not, because see, I am announcing to you good news of great joy for *all* the people: to you this day, in the city of David, was born a Savior, who is Messiah, the Lord." And he even gives us some directions, *(Shakes head in disbelief)* get this — "And this will be a sign to you. You will find the baby, having been wrapped up in cloths, lying in an animal feed box."

Well, I thought I had seen and heard it all at that point, and was glad I'd lived to tell the tale. But then, *(Pauses, filled with awe)* a whole army's worth of heavenly beings were with the messenger, and they were shouting and singing.

(Eli starts singing in his gruff voice, perhaps slightly off key. He claps his hands and stomps his feet, getting more and more into it)

    Glory to God in the highest
    And on earth peace among those whom God favors
    Glory to God in the ...

(Eli stops suddenly, realizing that he's singing in front of everyone and slightly embarrassed) Uh, but then again, mebbe I'm not the best one to try singing that song.

Carol   "Angels We Have Heard On High"

Well, they all left, and now we're all awake. Nahum, he's ecstatic, praising God with tears running down his face. Another shepherd with us, Judah, well, I'd never seen him be anything but tough and mean. He's an ornery old cuss. But he's scared. He's still shakin' and he doesn't know what to do.

Me? I think about it, and I say, "Let's do it. Let's go to Bethlehem and see for ourselves what's happened, that the Lord has made known to us."

So we head off into the night. I tell you, I was just standing over there. One year ago! *(Shakes head)* Unbelievable. *(Nods his head)* And it's funny, what I remember is that, after all that excitement, after all that noise, everything suddenly seemed real quiet.

Carol   "Silent Night"

So we head into the city, still wondering how exactly we're going to find where the baby is. Turns out it wasn't so hard at all. The night was real quiet, and most people were asleep in the upstairs of the houses. We just went to the home where there was some commotion downstairs, where they keep the animals. We peek in the window, and what we see ... well, what we see is amazing. There, just like we'd been told, was a newborn baby wrapped up in cloths and being laid down in a manger.

Carol   "Away In A Manger"

So we're just standing there, waiting outside the door. Judah's still scared and hanging back. Nahum seems overcome with emotion, and is praying under his breath. Me, I slowly go up to the man and the woman there. I don't know what to say. I say, "Pardon me, uh, Ma'am, uh, Sir, uh ... we've come to see the Savior, Messiah the Lord?" And they just look at each other, smile, and slowly nod, like they know what I'm talking about! And they show me this baby. *(Eli makes like he's receiving and cradling the baby in his arms. He is fighting back tears)* He's just this little baby, you know. With little fingers, and little toes. And ... it's the most beautiful thing I've ever seen. And I stand there holding him, and I just start loving the baby and thanking God.

And I think, what's ahead for this baby? I mean, it doesn't seem like he's going to be the sort of Messiah that Nahum's hoping for, being born here. Will he be a king? I'm kind of embarrassed to say it, but I found myself almost hoping that some day he will be a shepherd, like King David, and me. But I still don't know who he really is.

Carol   "What Child Is This?"

(Joyfully, hardly able to contain himself) When we leave, people in Bethlehem are waking up, and we can't help ourselves. We're telling our story to everyone we see. Even Judah! Ha! We run up to everyone! The Messiah is born! The Messiah is born! It's news of such great joy, that we want to, no, we *need* to share it, and we want everyone else to feel the joy we feel. We want everyone everywhere to come and see!

Carol   "O Come, All Ye Faithful"

Well, we get back to our flocks, and we start thinking. That old cuss Judah, he says he's going to change his ways, and become a servant of God. I think to myself that that would take a miracle, but then again I'd just learned to believe in miracles. And you know, Judah's kept his word to this day.

Nahum, he says he can't wait for the baby to grow up and deliver Israel.

But me, I can't get over the fact that he was lying there in a feed box, and God's messenger said it was for all people. So I'm thinking this is big. Bigger even than Israel's problems with Rome. I'm thinking this is good news of great joy for all the people.

Well, that's my story. It's one that I haven't stopped telling to people all year long. I hope that maybe it will become your story too. And one that you will want to share with others. Now I don't claim to understand it all, but I know that it is a story of God, and a story of love, and a story of joy. For me, that's enough. Me, I've got to tell how God touched my life. What about you? *(Eli pauses, looks straight at the congregation, then exits)*

Carol   "Go Tell It On The Mountain"

O Holy Night

A Service Of Story, Song, And Scripture On Christmas Eve

D. Andrew Richardson

In the beginning was the Word. From the ancient birth narratives to poetry and legends through the centuries no season seems to bring forth stories like Christmas. It is my hope that this service allows the voices of these authors to speak to us anew of the glory of Christ's birth.

I dedicate this service to my father who inspired in me a love of literature, to my family whose stories continue to unfold before me, and to the congregation of Humphrey Memorial, for welcoming me into their story of faith.

O Holy Night

A Christmas Eve Worship Service

Some say that ever 'gainst that season comes
Wherein our Savior's birth is celebrated,
The bird of dawning singeth all night long;
And then, they say, no spirit can walk abroad;
The nights are wholesome; then no planets strike,
No fairy takes, nor witch hath power to charm,
So hallow'd and so gracious is the time.
(Shakespeare — from *Hamlet*)

Prelude

Greeting and Announcements

Call to Worship (adapted from Thomas à Kempis)

One: O love, how deep, how broad how high, beyond all thought and fantasy. That God, the Son of God should take our mortal form for mortal's sake.

All: He sent no angel to our race, of higher or of lower place; but wore the robe of human frame, and to this work himself he came.

One: All glory to our Lord and God, for love so deep, so high, so broad. The trinity whom we adore forever and forever more.

In The Beginning Was The Word

Carol   "Hark! The Herald Angels Sing"

In The Beginning (Miriam Therese Winter)

Lighting of the Christ Candle

The Nativity

The Magnificat   Luke 1:46-55

Solo   "Ave Maria"

Prayer of Confession (adapted from a Mother's Union prayer)
Choosing God, choosing to let your child be born in poverty and of doubtful parenting. Choosing an occupied country with unstable rulers. Choosing the risk of his dying in a dirty stable after a long journey by a pregnant teenager. Choosing to let him grow up poor, and in danger and misunderstood by those who loved him. Choosing God, we doubt the wisdom of your choices then and we doubt them now while the rich are still full, and the poor sent empty away. Help us, lest we in our anger or ignorance choose to walk another way. Amen.

Words of Assurance

One: The baby born this night is an eternal sign that God is with us. Who can be against us? We are forgiven people!

All: Thanks be to God!

Choral Response   "Gloria" (Jacques Berthier)

Bethlehem (Bliss Carman)

Carol   "Still, Still, Still"

Sharon's Prayer (John Shea)

Carol   "See Amid The Winter's Snow"

Incarnation

Scripture   Colossians 1:15-20

Here It Begins

Carol   "In The Bleak Midwinter" (vv. 1-4)

The Work Of Christmas

A Hymn On The Nativity Of My Saviour (Ben Jonson)

Carol   "What Child Is This?"

And Now God Says To Us ... (Karl Rahner)

Carol   "It Came Upon A Midnight Clear"

The Birth Of Christ (Rainer Maria Rilke)

The Offering

Offertory   "In The Bleak Midwinter" (v. 5)

Christ Climbed Down (Lawrence Ferlinghetti)

Carol   "Silent Night, Holy Night"

Commissioning   If Ye Would Hear The Angels Sing (Dora Greenwell)

The Benediction

Postlude

Readings For The Service

Miriam Therese Winter is a poet, musician, and liturgist and is professor of liturgy, worship, and spirituality at Hartford Seminary. She is perhaps best known for her musical work with the Medical Mission Sisters and her song "Joy Is Like The Rain." This selection comes from *Woman Prayer/ Woman Song: Resources for Ritual.*

In The Beginning
In the beginning
before the mountains had been shaped,
before the hills,
before the beginning of the earth:
In the beginning,
before the birdsong
or the breath of life
lifted its gift
to the warmth of the sun:
In the beginning
was the Word
and the Word was with God
when God established the heavens,
when God drew a circle on the face of the deep,
when God marked out the foundations of the earth,
the Word was with God,
and the Word was God.
The Word was Power,
empowering all,
and the Word was Light,
enlightening all,
and the Word was Love,
loving all.
And the Word became flesh
and lived with us;
Ultimate Truth,
Source of Grace,
made of our world
a holy place,
and it was in the beginning
is now,
and shall be
always and forever.

Luke 1:39-55
The Magnificat
In those days Mary went with haste to a Judean town in the hill country, where she entered the house of Zechariah and greeted Elizabeth. And when Elizabeth heard the greeting of Mary, the babe leaped in her womb; and Elizabeth was filled with the Holy Spirit and she exclaimed with a loud cry, "Blessed are you among women, and blessed is the fruit of your womb! And why is this granted to me, that the mother of my Lord should come to me? For behold, when the voice of your greeting came to my ears, the babe in my womb jumped for joy. And blessed is she who believed that there would be a fulfillment of what was spoken to her from the Lord." And Mary said,
"My soul magnifies the Lord,
and my spirit rejoices in God my Savior,
for God has regarded the low estate of his handmaiden.
For behold, henceforth all generations will call me blessed;
for God who is mighty has done great things for me, and holy is God's name.
And God's mercy on those who fear him from generation to generation.
God has shown strength with his arm,
He has scattered the proud in the imagination of their hearts,
God has put down the mighty from their thrones,
and exalted those of low degree;
God has filled the hungry with good things,
and the rich he has sent empty away.
God has helped his servant Israel, in remembrance of his mercy,
as he spoke to our ancestors, to Abraham and his descendants forever."
And Mary remained with her three months, and then
returned to her home.

Canadian by birth, Bliss Carman (1861-1929) was both scholar and poet. This poem, based on a traditional French carol, first appeared in the magazine *Pictorial Review*.

Bethlehem
Long was the road to Bethlehem,
Where Joseph and Mary came.
They are travel-worn, the day grows late,
As they reach the town with its towered gate —
The city of David's royal line —
And the stars of eve are beginning to shine.
They must seek a place where the poor may rest,
For Mary is weary and overpressed.

AND IT IS THE SIXTH HOUR

They come to an inn and knock on the door,
Asking a little space — no more
Than a humble shelter in their need.

The innkeeper gives them scanty heed.
Little for strangers does he care —
His house is full. They must seek elsewhere.
Fearing to find no place that day,
Heavy at heart they turn away.

AND IT IS THE SEVENTH HOUR

In weariness and sore perplexed,
To a larger house they venture next.
Joseph for pity's sake begs again
A lodging for Mary in her pain.
They are poor Galileans, plain to be told —
Their garments are worn, their sandals are old.
The fat innkeeper jingles his keys,
And refuses shelter to such as these.

AND IT IS THE NINTH HOUR

Where now they turn the woman is kind,
The place is crowded, still she would find
Room for them somehow — moved at the sight
Of this gentle girl in her urgent plight,
Who tells of her hope and her strength far spent,
And seems to her woman's heart God-sent,
But the surly landlord roars in wrath
And sends them forth on their lonely path.

AND IT IS THE ELEVENTH HOUR

Still seeking a place to lay them down,
They come at length, on the edge of town,
To a cattle-shed with sagging door,
Thankful for only the stable floor,
When an old gray donkey crowds to the wall
To make them room in his straw-laid stall.
And the cattle low at the stifled wail
Of a woman's voice in sore travail.

IT IS MIDNIGHT AND MARY'S HOUR

Over the place a great new star
Sheds wonder and glory beheld afar,
While all through the height of heaven there flies
The word of a seraph voice that cries,
"Glory to God, this wondrous morn
On earth the Savior Christ is born."

John Shea is a theologian who has taught at Loyola University and Saint Mary of the Lake Seminary. He is known worldwide as a gifted storyteller. The poem "Sharon's Prayer" by John Shea is taken from the anthology *O Holy Night*, edited by A. Jean Lesher, Saint Mary's Press, Christian Brothers Publications, Winona, Minnesota.

Sharon's Prayer
She was five,
sure of the facts,
and recited them
with slow solemnity,
convinced every word
was revelation.
She said
they were so poor
they had only peanut butter and jelly
sandwiches to eat
and they went a long way from home
without getting lost. The lady rode
a donkey, the man walked, and the baby
was inside the lady.
They had to stay in a stable
with an ox and an ass but the
Three Rich Men found them
because a star lited the roof.
Shepherds came and you could
pet the sheep but not feed them.
Then the baby was borned.
And do you now who he was?
Her quarter eyes inflated
to silver dollars.

The baby was God!

And she jumped in the air,
whirled round, dove into the sofa,
and buried her head
under the cushion
which is the only proper response
to the Good News
of the Incarnation.

This reading was found in a Christmas letter from a Minnesota church office. The office thought its origin was a hymn sung by a college choir at a Christmas concert.

Here It Begins

Here it begins, in the dark before dawning.
Here, in a barn full of animal smells.
The warm breath of cattle, the sounds of the morning,
Here without tinsel or tolling of bells.

This is the Word Who was there at the Making?
This is the pure and unbearable Light?
Tiny and wrinkle-faced, squalling and shaking
Small fists at the vast and implacable night?

Who can believe this impossible fable?
And He is stronger than all our sins.
A light in the darkness, a child in the stable.
Stronger than death itself, here it begins.

Colossians 1:15-20

He is the image of the invisible God, the firstborn of all creation; for in him all things were created, in heaven and on earth, visible and invisible, whether thrones or dominions or principalities or authorities — all things were created through him and for him. He is before all things, and in him all things hold together. He is the head of the body, the Church; he is the beginning, the firstborn from the dead, and in everything he might be preeminent. For in him all fullness of God was pleased to dwell, and through him to reconcile to himself all things, whether on earth or in heaven, making peace by the blood of his cross.

Ben Jonson (1572-1637) was in effect England's first poet laureate and was also a noted dramatist.

A Hymn On The Nativity Of My Saviour

I sing the birth was born tonight,
The author both of life and light;
The angels so did sound it.
And like the ravished shepherds said,
Who saw the light and were afraid,
Yet searched, and true they found it.

The Son of God, the eternal king,
That did us all salvation bring,
And freed the soul from danger:
He whom the whole world could not take,
The Word, which heaven and earth did make,
Was now laid in a manger.

The Father's wisdom willed it so,
The Son's obedience knew no No,
Both wills were in one stature;
And as that wisdom had decreed,
The Word was now made flesh indeed,
And took on Him our nature.

What comfort by Him do we win,
Who made Himself the prince of sin,
To make us heirs of glory!
To see this babe all innocence,
A martyr born in our defence —
Can man forget the story?

Karl Rahner (1904-1984), a German Jesuit, was one of the foremost theologians of the twentieth century. He is famous for his volumes of systematic theology titled *Theological Investigations*.

And Now God Says To Us ...

And now God says to us what he has already said to the world as a whole through his grace-filled birth: "I am there. I am with you. I am your life. I am the gloom of your daily routine. Why will you not bear it? I weep at your tears — pour out yours to me, my child. I am your joy. Do not be afraid to be happy, for ever since I wept, joy is the standard of living that is really more suitable than the anxiety and grief of those who think they have no hope. I am the blind alleys of all your paths, for when you no longer know how to go any farther, then you have reached me, foolish child, though you are not aware of it. I am in your anxiety, for I have shared it by suffering it.

"This reality — incomprehensible wonder of my almighty love — I have sheltered safely in the cold stable of your world. I am there. I no longer go away from this world, even if you do not see me now ... I am there. It is Christmas. Light the candles. They have more right to exist than all the darkness. It is Christmas. Christmas that lasts forever."

Rainer Maria Rilke (1875-1926) is generally considered the greatest German poet since Goethe. This selection is from a collection called *The Life of the Virgin Mary*.

The Birth Of Christ

Hadst thou not simplicity, how should
that happen to thee which now lights up the night?
See, the God who rumbled over nations
makes himself mild and in thee comes into the world.

Hadst thou imagined him greater?

What is greatness? Right through all measures
that he crosses goes his straight destiny.

Even a star has no such path,
see thou, these kings are great,
and they draw before thy lap
treasures that they hold be to be greatest,
and thou art perhaps astonished at this gift:
but look into the folds of thy shawl,
how even now he has exceeded all.

All amber that one ships afar,
all ornament of gold and the aromatic spice
that spreads blurringly in the senses:
all this was of rapid brevity,
and who knows but one has regretted it.
But (thou wilt see): He brings joy.

Lawrence Ferlinghetti (b. 1919) is one of America's most widely read poets. During the '60s his City Lights Bookstore was a center for avant-garde literature. This selection is from his collection of poems *A Coney Island of the Mind*.

Christ Climbed Down
Christ climbed down
from His bare Tree
this year
and ran away to where
there were no rootless Christmas trees
hung with candycanes and breakable stars

Christ climbed down
from His bare Tree
this year
and ran away to where
there were no gilded Christmas trees
and no tinsel Christmas trees
and no tinfoil Christmas trees
and no pink plastic Christmas trees
and no gold Christmas trees
and no black Christmas trees
and no powderblue Christmas trees
hung with electric candles
and encircled by tin electric trains
and clever cornball relatives

Christ climbed down
from His bare Tree
this year
and ran away to where
no intrepid Bible salesman
covered the territory
in two-tone Cadillacs
and where no Sears Roebuck creches
complete with plastic babe in manger
arrived by parcel post
the babe by special delivery
and where no televised Wise Men
praised the Lord Calvert Whiskey

Christ climbed down
from His bare Tree
this year
and ran away to where
no fat handshaking stranger
in a red flannel suit
and a fake white beard
went passing himself off
as some sort of North Pole saint
crossing the desert to Bethlehem
Pennsylvania
in a Volkswagon sled
drawn by rollicking Adirondack reindeer
with German names
and bearing sacks of Humble Gifts
from Saks Fifth Avenue
for everybody's imagined Christ Child

Christ climbed down
from His bare Tree
this year
and ran away to where
no Bing Crosby carollers
groaned of a white Christmas
and where no Radio City angels
iceskated wingless
thru a winter wonderland
into a jinglebell heaven
daily at 8:30
with Midnight Mass matinees

Christ climbed down
from His bare Tree
this year
and softly stole away into
some anonymous Mary's womb again
where in the darkest night
of everybody's anonymous soul
He awaits again
an unimaginable
and impossibly
Immaculate Reconception
The very craziest
Of Second Comings

Dora Greenwell (1821-1882), a poet and hymn writer, is the author of the collection *A Present Heaven*, written in 1862.

If Ye Would Hear The Angels Sing
If ye would hear the angels sing
"Peace on earth and mercy mild,"
Think of him who was once a child,
On Christmas Day in the morning.

If ye would hear the angels sing,
Rise, and spread your Christmas fare;
'Tis merrier still the more that share,
On Christmas Day in the morning.

Rise, and bake your Christmas bread;
Christians, rise! the world is bare,
And blank, and dark with want and care,
Yet Christmas comes in the morning.

If ye would hear the angels sing,
Rise, and light your Christmas fire;
And see that ye pile the logs still higher
On Christmas Day in the morning.

Rise, and light your Christmas fire;
Christians, rise! the world is old,
And Time is weary, and worn, and cold,
Yet Christmas comes in the morning.

If ye would hear the angels sing,
Christians! see ye let each door
Stand wider than it e'er stood before,
On Christmas Day in the morning.

Rise, and open wide the door;
Christians, rise! the world is wide,
And many there be that stand outside,
Yet Christmas comes in the morning.

Contributors

Jeanne Mueller is the Education Director of the Maryland Agricultural Education Foundation. A former elementary teacher, Mueller is an educational consultant and frequently leads teacher training workshops. She is a graduate of Towson State University and Loyola College (Baltimore) with a master's degree in curriculum and instruction. Currently a member of First United Presbyterian Church in Westminster, Maryland, Mueller has been a Sunday school teacher and religious education director for several congregations. **Judith Hale Wood**, the illustrator of *Come! See What God Has Done*, attended the Maryland Institute of Art in Baltimore, and used her artistic ability professionally as an illustrator for the oceanography department at Johns Hopkins University. She currently resides in Kennett Square, Pennsylvania.

James H. Edgar is the pastor of First Presbyterian Church in Beacon, New York. A native of Yorkshire, England, Edgar received his B.A. degree from Wooster College and his B.D. degree from McCormick Theological Seminary. **Ellen L. Edgar** is a former biology teacher who currently works as a tax preparer. She received her education from Alma College and Canisius College.

Elizabeth Morris-Pierce began her studies to become a United Methodist pastor following a term as the Business Administrator of the New York State Grange. She served as an officer in the Salvation Army for five years, and during 29 years as a pastor's wife her various church positions have included secretary, choir director, organist, and Sunday school teacher. She and her husband, Rev. Norman Morris, were foster parents to sixteen children before adopting their daughter. Morris-Pierce is also the author of *Onward! Through The Fog!* (CSS).

Stephen A. Berger, who works for the State of New York in energy and communications regulation, received his B.S. and M.S. degrees from Rensselaer Polytechnic Institute. He is an active member of First United Methodist Church in East Greenbush, New York, where he has been a Sunday school teacher and served on several committees. As well as writing plays, Berger performs original contemporary Christian music with his duo Stirred, Not Shaken — short for "Stirred by His Word, not Shaken by the world."

Eulonda A. Dreher has been a schoolteacher, directed a Christian preschool, and is currently the Secretary/Treasurer of the East Central Illinois Baptist Association. A graduate of Southern Illinois University, Dreher has written children's curriculum for LifeWay Christian Resources of the Southern Baptist Convention, and several of her drama and program scripts have been published in LifeWay's *National Drama Service* and *Let's Worship* magazines. She is also the author for CSS of *An Advent Worship Service*.

Russell W. Dalton is the G. Ernest Thomas Professor of Christianity and Communication at United Theological Seminary in Dayton, Ohio. He also is the director of United's Master of Arts in Religious Communication degree program. Dalton holds degrees from Central Michigan University (B.A.), Gordon-Conwell Theological Seminary (M.Div.), Harvard Divinity School (Th.M.), and Union Theological Seminary and the Presbyterian School of Christian Education (Ed.D.). An ordained American Baptist minister, Dalton served several congregations prior to pursuing doctoral studies. He is the author of *Video, Kids, and Christian Education*, as well as numerous articles and columns for denominational magazines.

D. Andrew Richardson is a graduate of Dalhousie University (B.A.) and Atlantic School of Theology (M.Div.), both located in Halifax, Nova Scotia. Currently the pastor of Humphrey Memorial United Church (United Church of Canada) in Moncton, New Brunswick, Richardson also spent a year as a Thompson scholar at Columbia Theological Seminary.